COVENANT BIBLE STUDIES

Revelation
Hope for the World
in Troubled Times

Richard H. Lowery

faithQuest ◆ Brethren Press

Unless otherwise noted, scripture quotations are from the New Revised Stand-
ard Version of the Bible, copyrighted © 1989 by the National Council of
Churches of Christ in the USA, Division of Education and Ministry.

Cover photo of bittersweet by Don Ford

98   97   96   95   94   5   4   3   2   1

Library of Congress Cataloging-in-Publication Data

Lowery, R. H. (Richard H.)
    Revelation : hope for the world in troubled times / Richard H. Lowery.
        p.   cm. — (Covenant Bible study series)
    Includes bibliographical references.
    ISBN 0-87178-739-3 (pbk.)
    1. Bible. N.T. Revelation—Study and teaching. I. Title. II. Series.
    BS2825.5.L69 1994
    228'.007—dc20   93-45777

Manufactured in the United States of America

Contents

Foreword

The Covenant Bible Study Series was first developed for a denominational program in the Church of the Brethren and the Christian Church (Disciples of Christ). This program, called People of the Covenant, was founded on the concept of relational Bible study and has been adopted by several other denominations and small groups who want to study the Bible in a community rather than alone.

Relational Bible study is marked by certain characteristics, some of which differ from other types of Bible study. For one, it is intended for small groups of people who can meet face-to-face on a regular basis and share frankly with an intimate group.

It is important to remember that relational Bible study is anchored in covenantal history. God covenanted with people in Old Testament history, established a new covenant in Jesus Christ, and covenants with the church today.

Relational Bible study takes seriously a corporate faith. As each person contributes to study, prayer, and work, the group becomes the real body of Christ. Each one's contribution is needed and important. "For just as the body is one and has many members, and all the members of the body, though many, are one body, so it is with Christ. . . . Now you are the body of Christ and individually members of it" (1 Cor. 12:12, 17).

Relational Bible study helps both individuals and the group to claim the promise of the Spirit and the working of the Spirit. As one person testified, "In our commitment to one another and in our sharing, something happened. . . . We were woven together in love by the master Weaver. It is something that can happen only when two or three or seven are gathered in God's name, and we know the promise of God's presence in our lives."

The symbol for these covenant Bible study groups is the burlap cross. The interwoven threads, the uniqueness of each strand, the unrefined fabric, and the rough texture characterize covenant groups. The people in the groups are unique but interrelated; they are imperfect and unpolished, but loving and supportive.

The shape that these divergent threads create is the cross, the symbol for all Christians of the resurrection and presence with us of Christ our Savior. Like the burlap cross, we are brought together, simple and ordinary, to be sent out again in all directions to be in the world.

For people who choose to use this study in a small group, the following guidelines will help create an atmosphere in which support will grow and faith will deepen.

1. As a small group of learners, we gather around God's word to discern its meaning for today.
2. The words, stories, and admonitions we find in scripture come alive for today, challenging and renewing us.
3. All people are learners and all are leaders.
4. Each person will contribute to the study, sharing the meaning found in the scripture and helping to bring meaning to others.
5. We recognize each other's vulnerability as we share out of our own experience, and in sharing we learn to trust others and to be trustworthy.

Additional suggestions for study and group-building are provided in the "Sharing and Prayer" section. They are intended for use in the hour preceding the Bible study to foster intimacy in the covenant group and relate personal sharing to the Bible study topic.

Welcome to this study. As you search the scriptures, may you also search yourself. May God's voice and guidance and the love and encouragement of brothers and sisters in Christ challenge you to live more fully the abundant life God promises.

Preface

In our democratic society, we like to say that we value every person. The rocket scientist is not better than the construction worker and the philosopher is not better than the custodian. But sometime in our lives we've all felt as if we weren't good enough. Surely you've attended a wedding or social function where you were underdressed compared to everyone else. Or you've been embarrassed to have your co-workers over for a picnic because your house is too modest. Or maybe you've been made to feel, even though you're biblically literate, as if you couldn't even read the Revelation to John because it's so mysterious that only your very religious friends seem to know what it means for sure.

We shouldn't worry. Insecure Christians in every age have been made to feel very small in the presence of their self-assured brothers and sisters in the faith. For example, groups such as the gnostics in the early years of Christianity claimed to have a special understanding of God and, therefore, to be superior in faith. Through mystical experience they transcended the ignorance and messiness of this life and drew nearer to the divine. Then they reserved for themselves a status far above ordinary people of faith who, as they saw it, only blindly accepted Jesus. We are not alone.

We don't read Revelation often, because it feels like a put-down. We feel as if we're spiritually inferior when we don't understand it and less a Christian for it. We wish we had the confidence of some who rejoice in Revelation's glorious victory over the forces of evil in this world, knowing they are on the right side of the struggle. We are the people for whom this study of Revelation is written, the insecure student, the people with Revelation anxiety. Author Rick Lowery takes Revelation back from the privileged and gives it to every sinner in the Christian faith.

Revelation, Lowery says, is not just about the victory of heaven over earth; it is hope in our times for an imperfect world. In its own time, the Revelation to John gave real hope to Christians who faced uncertainty and persecution. They were not so different from Christians today. They had no more virtue or blessing than we. And Revelation was not a promise of a glorious future to pacify Christians so they would wait patiently for their reward in heaven. It was powerful hope that brought real forces of good to bear in their lives and kept them from giving up or committing suicide to escape pain and suffering.

Situations change and issues vary, but every age faces troubled times. Revelation teaches us how to live in our miserable world with steadfastness and Christian hope. Assured of grace for our imperfections, we know that Christ comes even for us. Everyone who is thirsty may drink. That is all we need to know.

Julie Garber
Editor

Recommended Resources:

Barclay, William. *Revelation of John*, Vols. 1, 2. Louisville, Ky.: Westminster John Knox, 1976.

Boring, M. Eugene. *Revelation* (Interpretation Series). Louisville, Ky.: Westminster John Knox, 1989.

Wieand, David J. *Visions of Glory*. Elgin, Ill.: Brethren Press, 1979.

1

Let Those Who Have Ears Hear
Revelation 1:1-8

The language of Revelation is highly symbolic and difficult to understand. Originally written for a church in social and political danger, the message of Revelation is best heard today with the ears of those who are oppressed.

Personal Preparation

1. Revelation 1:3 promises a blessing on those who read the words of this book aloud and those who hear it. Alone or with others, read the whole book out loud.
2. Did you ever have a revelation? Think about events in your life that you've come to believe had a deeper significance than was apparent at the time they happened. What leads you to that conclusion?
3. Pray for understanding as you enter this study of Revelation.

Understanding

Have you ever visited a church service where you couldn't figure out what to do when? Worship may have seemed chaotic, the congregation suddenly standing or kneeling, shaking hands, raising hands, or speaking back when spoken to from the pulpit. Everyone else seemed to know when to do what, but you couldn't crack the code. Sometimes worship cues are conscious and formal: "The Lord be with you," the minister may say. "And also with you," the congregation knows to respond. Sometimes the cues are unspoken and maybe even unconscious.

When, after years of study in a divinity school, I returned to my "non-liturgical" home church in the South, I was struck by the fact that we, too, had an unspoken code. All at once toward the end of the sermon, virtually all 700 people reached for their hymnals to find the invitation song. No instruction was given from the pulpit. No ritual sentence was uttered. But everyone knew when the preacher was moving to the evangelistic call that concludes sermons in that tradition.

Consciously or not, all groups develop codes—words or gestures that make sense to those inside the group but mean something different or nothing at all to outsiders. Some codes are easy to decipher by an able observer. Some are completely obscure. But all codes communicate something intelligible to people in the know, while "hiding" something from everyone else.

The book of Revelation is coded communication. The English title of the book is taken from its first word, *apokalypsis*, in Greek, or *revelatus*, in Latin. It means "that which is uncovered." The information in this book is hidden to most but uncovered to those who have ears to hear (2:7). Notice that this is "the revelation of Jesus Christ, which God gave him to show his servants what must soon take place" (1:1). The revelation originates with God, is passed through Jesus to an angel, to John, and finally to God's servants. This revelation uncovers information about the very near future. It tells those who understand its code that the unfolding events of the present have a deeper meaning than meets the eye. They serve a grand and hidden purpose of God.

Many people have viewed Revelation as a vision of the end times when the world will be no more. But Revelation is actually the vision of what God will do in the world and how God will act in human affairs rather than divine ones. In this way, it is the vision of the beginning, a time when God will intervene and make a new thing happen, rather than a vision of the end. Revelation tells us God is doing something *in* the world, not *to* the world from afar.

The Hebrew Scriptures have various opinions about the way God acts in history. Sometimes God is said to intervene in astonishing ways—parting the sea, appearing in lightning and thunder at Mt. Sinai, giving audible instructions to chosen people. In other cases, such as the stories of Joseph (Gen. 37—50) and Ruth, God's action is so subtle it is virtually invisible. In some literature, such as Esther, Ecclesiastes, and many of the Proverbs, God is the object of devotion but does not intervene in history at all. In all of these views, God responds to human choices to rebel against the divine will.

A couple of centuries before Jesus was born, Israel developed yet another view of the way God acts in history. This time Hebrew thought was influenced by Zoroastrian religion of the Persians and the religious traditions of Greek culture. (The Persians liberated the exiled Jews from Babylonia in 538 B.C. and ruled Palestine until Greek imperial rule took over in 332 B.C.) The Persian and Greek religions portrayed a two-storied universe: heaven, where divine history transpires, and earth, the arena of human history. According to Zoroastrian religious texts, a battle rages in the heavenly realm between good and evil, fought by a host of angels and demons in the service of God and the devil. The ups and downs of human history and the good and evil that people do are reflections of that heavenly battle.

The book of Daniel uses elements of these Zoroastrian and Greek world views. And Daniel, like Revelation, is also an apocalyptic vision, a vision that reveals the hidden significance of the Hebrews' present suffering.

Daniel receives heavenly revelations in the form of dreamy visions. In them, Daniel sees bizarre creatures—a lion with eagles' wings, an arrogant horn that talks and rips stars from the sky, a giant ram and unicorn goat whose savage battle shakes the earth. But these fantastic creatures, Daniel's heavenly guide explains (8:18-26; 11:2-45), are symbolic of human political history from the time of Persian rule through the rule of the Greek King Antiochus IV (175-164 B.C.). Antiochus persecuted Jews and desecrated the Jerusalem temple, erecting an altar to Zeus and forbidding Jewish worship there (Dan. 8:11-13; 11:31). The symbolic visions of the book culminate with this persecution of the Jews (11:32-35) and announce that the arrogant king soon will be overthrown (11:45). In the meantime, the faithful will endure "a time of anguish, such as has never occurred since nations first came into existence" (12:1). Their suffering, however, will signal the end of history (12:1-3), when the faithful will be delivered and the dead resurrected and judged (12:2). This human history is a pale reflection of the cosmic battle between good and evil. The persecution under

Antiochus merely plays out the last scene of a script already completed in heaven, with God's forces victorious (7:9-15).

It is important to understand that whoever published the book of Daniel believed they were living in the end time: "But you, Daniel, keep the words secret and the book sealed until the time of the end" (12:4). For those who first read the book, the final deliverance seemed to be at hand. It is also important to realize that the book is coded so that "none of the wicked shall understand, but those who are wise shall understand" (12:10). Daniel offered the faithful a word of hope that their suffering had a deeper meaning, hidden from the powers that oppressed them. Their distress marked the end of time and, with it, the end of an unjust political order.

Like Daniel, Revelation is coded communication offered to the faithful who are living under the harsh conditions of persecution at the end of time. It offers insight into the deeper meaning of the church's suffering. Its images are bizarre and symbolic. Its language is intelligible to those in the know and mystifying to those on the outside who persecute the faithful. Its scope is not just global (1:7), but cosmic, encompassing all of history, heaven and earth, beginning to end: " 'I am the Alpha and the Omega' [the first and last letters of the Greek alphabet, from A to Z], says the Lord God, 'who is and who was and who is to come' " (1:8). It speaks not to a distant future, but explains to John (1:1) and his first-century Christian audience in Asia (1:4) the hidden significance of "what must soon take place" (1:1). For them "the time is near" (1:3) for the revelation's fulfillment.

Though Revelation speaks to the situation of churches under Roman persecution at the end of the first century, Christians throughout history have heard in this book a divine word of hope in times of distress. As coded language, Revelation lends itself to controversy and a wide variety of interpretation. It is usually most meaningful to those who see the social-political order as oppressive and corrupt, in need of radical reform or outright destruction. Generally, Christians who are satisfied with the status quo have ignored Revelation or treated it with suspicion. For example, the Christian revolutionary Thomas Münzer (1489-1525) based his radical social-religious program on Revelation. But Bishop Eusebius, a confidant of Emperor Constantine (fourth century), expressed doubts about including it in the New Testament.

For Christians living in basic economic security, free of governmental or social persecution, Revelation may seem unrelated to everyday life. It may even frighten rather than reassure. To get the full impact of Revelation and the blessing it promises (1:3), Christians living in relatively comfortable circumstances need to listen to its message with the ears of the persecuted, those on the bottom side of the social order. The key to its code lies in deep empathy with those who find little hope in the way things are. For this reason, a proper reading requires a global perspective and a strong sense of the church's fundamental unity across national and class barriers. When one member suffers, all suffer. Even those of us who, thank God, suffer little can listen if we have ears that can hear. Blessed are we if we can crack the code, find meaning in the chaos, and find a deep and wonderful word of hope.

Discussion and Action

1. Take turns reading today's passage aloud, preferably from different translations. Pay attention to the differences in the translations.
2. Discuss a time when God has taken an active hand in your life. What is it about the thing that happened that makes you certain God intervened? Keep a list of the group's experiences and reasons for thinking God was at work. Are there common experiences? similar reasons for thinking God was at work? Based on your discussion, what are some things to look for to determine how God works in your personal life? in larger social and political events?
3. Name some ways in which the church is persecuted today.
4. Name some things in recent history or in the world today for which the church ought to risk persecution. What might your church do to take a risk for the sake of the gospel?
5. Karl Marx is infamous for having said that religion "is the opium of the people." Is Revelation just an addictive painkiller to keep us comfortable in a sick society? How might religion spur us to seek a cure?
6. The publishers of Daniel thought they lived in "the time of the end" (12:4). The author of Revelation (likely John) told his first-century audience that "the time is near" (1:3), that Jesus is "coming soon" (22:20). Were they wrong? Are they right in some sense? Is it possible to say that we, like

they, are living in the time of the end? If you knew the world
were about to end, what would you do differently?

7. In your next worship service, try to think like a visitor who
    is unfamiliar with the way things are done and what they
    mean. Where is your worship coded? Which of that coding
    is appropriate? inappropriate?

2

A Vision of Christ in the Church's Night
Revelation 1:9-20

John receives the vision during worship, while he is "in the spirit on the Lord's day." He has been exiled to the island of Patmos, "because of . . . the testimony of Jesus." Living in Christ sometimes puts Christians in conflict with the larger social and political powers. But worshipful focus on the presence of God in our midst gives us strength to persevere.

Personal Preparation
1. Read today's passage aloud at least twice a day for a week.
2. John's vision comes during a dream. Think of other important messages in the Bible that came through dreams and visions. Look up some of these to share with your group.
3. Think about dreams you've had that obviously spoke to a critical situation you faced in your waking hours.
4. Consider keeping a dream log in which you write down your dreams. Keep a notebook and pen at your bedside, and write as much as you remember as soon as you wake up.

Understanding
Dreams, Sigmund Freud thought, hold the key to the unconscious. A proper understanding of them can help us figure out why we act

the way we do when we are awake. They can help us remember and come to terms with painful things we may have hidden from our conscious memory. Proper understanding of our dreams can help us lead happier lives, Freud believed. Whatever the validity of Freudian analysis, his insight surely is right that dreams often speak our innermost thoughts and deal with the difficulties and delights we face in our waking hours. Dreams properly heard and understood can reveal deep truth.

The importance Freud attached to dreams was nothing new. Biblical heroes from Jacob to Joseph, from Mary to Peter, had revelations in their dreams that changed the course of history. Whether a heavenly ramp, an angelic visitation, or a tablecloth bearing an unkosher feast, biblical dreams speak of a divine reality that touches the everyday world. The symbols in those dreams are sometimes bizarre but always rooted in things we see and feel and touch in our daily lives. When Pharaoh dreamed that puny cows gobbled up big beefy ones (Gen. 41:20), Joseph and Pharaoh both knew that the dream signaled desolation and famine which sometimes follow seemingly endless bounty. Sub-Saharan Africa and Russia's dried-up Aral Sea are grim reminders of this deep truth. Real-world living is the stuff dreams are made of.

The revelation given to John is dreamlike. Its strange imagery grows out of the everyday reality faced by the churches to which he writes in the late first century. But it is a deeper vision that pierces the surface of everyday life and also grasps the divine reality undergirding it.

John receives his vision while he is "in the spirit on the Lord's day" (1:10). Though exiled on Patmos, he continues to observe Sunday worship, a custom which joins him with Christians elsewhere. His worship puts him "in the spirit." These visible acts of praise seem to transport John in a different place, the invisible realm of the spirit where he received his vision. His experience would be much like our experience with deep prayer.

The loud trumpetlike voice that announces John's vision (1:10) instructs him to write what he sees and to send it to seven churches (1:11) in the Roman province of Asia (modern Turkey). Though transmitted through one person, John, God's revelation is intended for the corporate church. The real-life situations of these seven churches is the starting point of John's heavenly vision. But the dream is a reflection of both an earthly reality of pain and perse-cution and a heavenly reality of hope.

Immediately John sees seven golden lampstands. In their midst stands a bright human-looking being (1:13-15) who holds seven stars in his right hand (1:16). Like Daniel and Ezekiel before him, John falls in a dead faint at this awesome sight (1:17). The heavenly being revives him and reveals himself as "the first and the last" (cf. God in 1:8). "I am . . . the living one," the being says, "I was dead, and see, I am alive forever and ever; and I have the keys of Death and of Hades" (1:18). It is Jesus, crucified, risen, and exalted, who addresses John.

Many images in the beginning of the dream connect earth and heaven. The seven lampstands, he explains, are the seven churches, and the seven stars are the churches' angels. The risen Jesus stands in their midst, though in everyday life they do not see him. Each church has an angel attached to it. Over and over, the heavenly realm touches the earthly (as corporate communities, not isolated indi-viduals). These images demonstrate that what the churches experi-ence is not merely this-worldly. It is joined to the heavenly.

The opening words of today's passage reveal the two aspects of reality in which John and the churches are living: "I, John, your brother who shares with you in Jesus the persecution and the kingdom and the patient endurance" (1:9). On the one hand the church faces the tangible reality of persecution and, on the other, the intangible but very real dominion of God. It is no accident, in this verse, that political persecution and God's dominion are joined. John's exile on Patmos is "because of the word of God and the testimony of Jesus." He was persecuted for his faith. For John, to live in God's dominion is to suffer persecution. But it is precisely because of the reality of God's reign that John and others are able to persevere. Those who are "in Jesus" find patient endurance in the conviction that God is in control, even in times of distress. Heavenly reality makes sense of earthly suffering and gives courage to go on.

The movie *Romero* offers a modern-day example of conflict between political interests and God's dominion. It shows the patient endurance that can arise when people are persecuted for their faith. The movie documents the life of Salvadoran Bishop Oscar Romero from the time he became Archbishop of San Salvador until he was assassinated while lifting the communion cup in celebration of mass. Initially considered a "safe" moderate by the aristocratic military junta that ruled the country, Romero found himself more and more distressed by the plight of the poor and the deadly tactics of the National Guard. As priests and church workers increasingly were targeted for arrest, torture, and assassination, Romero became more and more outspoken in his opposition to the military regime.

One of the most powerful moments in the movie comes when Romero drives into a city where National Guardsmen have gutted and occupied a church that they considered to be a center of "subversive" activity. When he demands that the church be reopened, Romero is threatened and thrown out. With his aide, he reenters the church to recover the communion wafers which have been thrown on the floor by the occupiers. To the soldiers, the wafers were worthless bread. To Romero, they contained the presence of Christ. As he bends down to pick up the bread, one of the soldiers releases a hail of machine gun fire just over Romero's head, shooting up the front part of the church, including the eucharistic table.

Visibly shaking, Romero rushes out of the church with as many of the wafers as he can hold. He and his aide get into their car and drive off. But only a couple of minutes later, their car returns. Romero gets out, now wearing his priestly stole. Holding a cross above his head, he walks toward the church where the soldiers now amass at the door with weapons pointed toward him. Quietly, the townspeople begin to step in behind Romero as he heads up to and through the line of soldiers into the church to celebrate mass. In this case, the presence of Christ in the communion bread becomes the occasion for the church's persecution and, in the end, gives Christians the courage to persevere, though threatened and afraid.

Sometimes, in the midst of crisis, the church gets a clear vision of Christ among us. People of faith do the right thing, suffer for it, and keep on doing the right thing. They catch a vision that helps them see beyond the danger and persevere. For the churches of Asia whom John addressed, the inspiration was the vision of Jesus, crucified and raised, standing in their midst even as they suffered persecution. The one who had triumphed over death now stood with them as they faced death for his sake. These moments of revelation still occur when people of faith, like Romero in the Salvadoran church building, like John in worship on Patmos, or like Jacob when he woke from his dream at Bethel, suddenly realize that "surely the Lord is in this place—and I did not know it!" (Gen. 28:16).

Discussion and Action

1. Report back to the group the "codes" you found used in your congregation's worship. Discuss how some of these codes are not welcoming to visitors. What follow-up action might you take?
2. "Living in Christ sometimes puts Christians in conflict with the larger social and political powers." Remember the young Chinese man who stopped a column of tanks in Tiananmen Square? Who won that standoff? Why?
3. Name some other situations where a ray of hope has shone out of a seemingly hopeless situation.
4. Where do you see Jesus in today's church? in the world?
5. Has worship ever put you in danger? Has worship ever rescued you from danger?
6. If possible, watch and discuss the movie *Romero*. Or have someone who has seen the movie talk about it with your group.

3

Rendering to Caesar
Revelation 2:1—3:22

First-century Christians were required by law to participate in ritual meals at shrines to the Roman deities "Caesar" and "Roma." Some Christians urged participation rather than martyrdom. After all, the idols were just dead wood and cold stone. They had no real meaning. But John calls such compromise "fornication" and urges Christians to die rather than go through the motions of the imperial cult. As the church today, we must examine the compromises we make with the cultural "idols" around us.

Personal Preparation
1. Read Revelation 2 and 3 aloud, imagining you are reading these words in a letter your church just received.
2. Think of a symbol to describe your church and the reason for choosing that particular symbol. Plan to explain the symbol.
3. Keep your dream log. Try to figure out how your dreams relate to your waking life.
4. Think of a time in the recent past when you have been faced with the decision to compromise a belief or your faith.

Understanding

In the movie *The Wizard of Oz*, a bump on the head during a violent windstorm leaves Dorothy unconscious. While asleep Dorothy has a dream, which carries her far from her Kansas home to a strange land somewhere over the rainbow. As the characters of Oz appear, however, they bear a striking resemblance to folks back home. The three farmhands who help run the homestead are transformed into Dorothy's three companions on the Yellow Brick Road—Scarecrow, Tin Man, and Cowardly Lion. The traveling showman becomes the all-too-human wizard. Most striking is the grouchy neighbor who in real life tried to destroy Dorothy's dog, Toto. As Dorothy's house spins up in the funnel of the tornado, Dorothy sees her cruel neighbor fly by the window, furiously peddling her bicycle. A horrified Dorothy watches the neighbor gradually change into a frightening witch and her bicycle, into a flying broom.

Revelation is neither a Hollywood movie nor the strange hallucination of someone hit on the head. But it does use a literary technique very much like the cinematic technique in *The Wizard of Oz*. The heavenly visions John sees are transformed images of down-to-earth church history in the late first century. The letters to the churches in Revelation 2 and 3 are part of the heavenly vision which began in 1:10. They speak in otherworldly terms, but also talk about this-worldly struggles the churches faced. These chapters are a turning point in the book, bridging the earthly and heavenly realities the revelation describes. To use the movie analogy, these chapters are the part where John and the reader spin around in the funnel cloud, watching the churches' flesh-and-blood enemies begin to change into the otherworldly spiritual enemies of the heavenly visions that follow. To understand the beasts and dragons, the mothers, martyrs, and "whores" that appear later, we must pay close attention to what was happening to the Asian churches in those days.

Jesus tells John to write seven letters to the seven angels of the Asian churches (2:1, 8, 12, 18; 3:1, 7, 14). The letters describe threats from without and within and urge the churches to stand fast. Their patient endurance will "conquer" that which threatens them, leading them to life everlasting.

The threats grew out of larger religious and political circumstances. The Roman empire tolerated the religions of the people it ruled. As a sign of patriotic loyalty, however, Roman subjects were required to worship the imperial deities: Roma, the goddess of heaven, and Caesar, the deified emperor. Most people at that time were polytheistic, worshiping a number of different gods. Adding the gods of Rome made little difference to them. It posed a big problem, however, for a monotheistic religion such as Judaism. In recognition of this, the Romans exempted Jews from the legal requirement to worship Roman deities.

Early on, Christians were also exempted from paying homage to Roman gods, because they were considered Jewish (Acts 2:22-36, 46; 5:33-39). As time passed, however, Christianity became a distinct religion, with an increasingly non-Jewish membership. As Christianity separated itself, hot debates flared between church and synagogue. It was like what happens when teenagers begin to separate themselves from their parents and establish their own independent identity. Church and synagogue exchanged harsh words and did hurtful things. The separation was mutual, but it carried a high political price for Christians.

The letters to Smyrna (2:8-11) and Philadelphia (3:7-13) describe churches in the middle of this separation from the synagogue and suggest that they were about to suffer political persecution for it. Apparently in these two cities Jewish leaders were distancing themselves from Christians. They were making it clear to the Roman authorities that Christianity was now a distinct, non-Jewish religion. John calls their actions "slander" and describes them as "a synagogue of Satan" (2:9-10; 3:9). He warns that Christians soon will be imprisoned and executed by Rome, which he describes as "the devil" (2:10). Eventually Christians lost the exemption from patronizing the imperial cults and were persecuted by the state.

Limited persecution already had begun by the time Revelation was written (2:9, 13), but John could see the handwriting on the wall. Things would and did get worse. About twenty years later, Roman officials there were using torture to extract confessions and issuing death sentences to those who refused to recant faith in Christ and make offerings to the Roman gods. The Romans were not going out looking for Christians, but when Christians came through the judicial system, they were dealt with harshly.

Additionally, the church faced an internal threat. John's letters to the churches make cryptic references to false apostles (2:2), "Nicolaitans" (2:6, 15), those "who hold to the teaching of Balaam" (2:14), a "Jezebel" prophet (2:20), and "lukewarm" Christians who are "neither cold nor hot" (3:15-16). The key problem seems to be that Christians were participating in ritual meals for idols (2:14, 20). Apparently, according to John's opponents, Christians could take part in imperial rituals while remaining faithful to Christ. But John says his opponents are teaching fellow Christians "to practice fornication and to eat food sacrificed to idols" (2:20). Fornication, in this context, probably refers to the frequent descriptions in the Bible of Israel's idol worship as "adultery" (Deut. 31:16; Judg. 2:17). John describes the churches' idolatry as "the deep things of Satan" (2:24). Having already identified Rome with "the devil" (2:10), John seems to be talking about the imperial cult.

Since the time of Paul, Christians had wrestled with this issue. Some Corinthian Christians argued that it was fine to participate in ritual meals in the temple of an idol, because "no idol in the world really exists" and "there is no God but one" (1 Cor. 8:4). Besides, "for us there is one God . . . from whom are all things and for whom we exist, and one Lord, Jesus Christ" (8:6). Therefore, Christians could do their patriotic duty to Caesar and Roma without violating their Christian conscience, because they knew in their own minds that the idols and rituals were meaningless. It is as if Christians could say "I had my fingers crossed!" to absolve themselves of idolatry. Paul is sympathetic to the reasoning of these knowledgeable Christians (8:7, 10, 11), but he warns them against letting their "liberty" become "a stumbling block to the weak" who object to Christian participation in the imperial cult (8:9-13).

The "knowledgeable" Christians Paul describes and the "fornicating idol worshipers" John condemns are actually the Christian moderates, who sought a conscientious compromise with imperial culture. Perhaps they conformed to save their own skins or to keep the church from being destroyed or to preserve some kind of influence in Roman society. Whatever their motives, they believed they were staking out an acceptable Christian position. John, however, rejects their accommodation with imperial culture and considers it a threat as great as that of persecution.

Martin Luther King, Jr.'s "Letter from Birmingham Jail" deals with the same issue. King was criticized by white "moderate" pastors who expressed sympathy with the goal of desegregation, but condemned King's violation of segregationist laws. A more accommodating, less confrontational approach would be more effective, these white moderates argued. Besides, as Romans 13 and 1 Peter 2 state, Christians should obey the law of the land because God is the one who puts governments in power and allows them to rule. From his jail cell, King penned a response in the tradition of Revelation, a ringing indictment of racist America and a hope-filled call to uncompromising resistance.

Christians living under government oppression have found courage and hope in King's letter and in John's revelation. We heard it in the soon-to-be-martyred Archbishop Romero's appeal to the Salvadoran National Guard to lay down their weapons and stop the killing. We saw it in unflinching opposition to apartheid by South African Christians. We watched it as a tiny Christian church in East Germany catalyzed a nonviolent uprising that brought down the Berlin Wall.

Few of us in the U.S. and Canada today experience the kind of government persecution John or King or Romero knew. We seldom face the choice of obeying God or obeying the law. But everyday we are confronted with the decision to compromise with powerful and sometimes anti-Christian cultural forces.

For instance, as Christians we live in cities that are powderkegs of racial tension. And racial segregation finds its way into churches across the land every Sunday. Few congregations exhibit much energy for common worship, fellowship, and local mission work with Christians of different ethnic heritage. All too often we stay with "birds of a feather" as does the larger culture, building Christian community around racial, educational, and socio-economic sameness. This worldly wisdom does little to address the racism that runs rampant and, in the worst case, leads to racist violence and "ethnic cleansing."

Likewise, in a thousand ways, the culture tells men that they have the right to control women; and it tells women that sex appeal is their chief value, their surest route to happiness, and that guileful manipulation of men is their only access to power. This sexist message has caused a social and spiritual crisis of disease, unwanted pregnancy, and rape, rooted in promiscuous and violent sexual relationships. Yet churches all too often participate in this same behavior, excluding women from official power, giving them only an unofficial, behind-the-scenes voice. When do our compromises make us accomplices to evil?

Revelation issues a clear call in a crisis moment: no compromise! But to those who stand firm, who suffer the consequences of unyielding faith, the risen Jesus gives access to the tree of life (2:7). No two-bit wizard in a land of hallucinations, Jesus offers life everlasting to those who keep the faith. Let anyone who has an ear listen to what the Spirit is saying to the churches (3:13)!

Discussion and Action

1. Discuss the difficult situation facing the early Christian church and the Christian's temptation to compromise his or her faith. In your view, was compromise justified? Why or why not?

2. Read Romans 13:1-7 and 1 Peter 2:11-17. How do you think John would have responded?

3. When have you found your own Christian conscience in conflict with policies of the government? Can you imagine any circumstances in which you might have to choose between being a patriotic, law-abiding citizen and being faithful to God?

4. When I was a child, a neighbor believed that television— not the specific programming, but the technology itself— was "of the devil." At the same time several people in my church believed that dancing, playing cards, and "mixed bathing" (i.e., people of both sexes swimming in the same pool) were utterly sinful. Very few people, even in that church, hold such opinions any longer. Are there things your church now tolerates or even encourages that would cause your grandparents in the faith to "roll over in their graves"? What are some things you have changed your mind about—things you once thought were wrong or questionable, but which now seem okay? What made you change your mind? Have you simply compromised with culture? Are all compromises bad? Give examples.

5. Write a letter exhorting yourself and your church in the tradition of Revelation.

6. What techniques or symbols or technologies have Christians adopted from the broader culture and turned to good use in the churches? What are the risks involved in doing that?

4

Being There
Revelation 4:1—5:14

John's vision of heaven begins with the resurrected Jesus standing in the midst of the persecuted churches. In the here-and-now, he is invisible. "In the Spirit," he can be seen standing with the churches. Even in the midst of this revelation, however, some things remain hidden. Our confidence comes not from knowledge of the future, but from the presence of God who is willing and able to save.

Personal Preparation

1. Read chapters 4 and 5 aloud, chanting the parts where the heavenly creatures sing.
2. Sing some of your favorite hymns of praise and adoration, or listen to recordings of majestic songs of praise through the week.
3. Read Exodus 25:10-22, Isaiah 6, and Ezekiel 1—3 as background. Note the images similar to ones in Revelation 4 and 5: the throne room, cherubims, serafims, movement, and music. How is God present in each of these scriptures? How do you know that God is present in the life of your church?

Understanding

"What's going to happen? Will everything be all right?" Those of us who have faced life-threatening illness in ourselves or a loved one know the agony of waiting. It seems like an eternity from the time the doctor first notices something wrong until the test results are in. The uncertainty of the wait seems worse than the bad news we might get. Lingering on the edge of the unknown can be frightening and is always spiritually draining.

Often we are uncomfortable being with people in these uncertain moments of crisis, because we don't know what to say. We don't have a satisfying answer to their (and our) questions: What's going to happen to me? Will I be all right? The truth is, we cannot say for sure what will happen. The afflicted person may die soon. The survivor may be devastated. It is disconcerting that we cannot predict the future, when the future is what we most want to know.

In times of crisis, we may not know what to say, but we can offer hope and comfort just by being present. As a student pastor several years ago, I regularly visited a beautiful, joyful woman, homebound by terminal cancer. Toward the end of the summer, she moved into the final stages of her disease and was taken to a hospital. When I walked into intensive care that last day, I was stunned to see her hooked to machines through a maze of tubes and electrodes. She couldn't speak or smile her beautiful smile—the respirator wouldn't allow that. She looked scared. I was terrified.

Sitting next to her, I took her hand and began to read from the Bible I'd brought: "The Lord is my shepherd, I shall not want . . . " "I am convinced that neither death nor life . . . nor anything else in all creation can separate us from the love of God . . . . " I said aloud that I knew she was scared and that I was scared, but God was with us now and would be with us whatever happened. I asked her to pray the Lord's Prayer with me, just like we always did when we visited. She couldn't speak, but she squeezed my hand tight as I repeated the familiar words. Then I quietly held her hand until she fell asleep. I couldn't tell her what the next few hours would hold, but I could offer her a hand to hold and a common faith in the God who walks with us, even when we walk through the valley of the shadow of death. Hope is found in presence, not prediction.

Revelation 4 and 5 celebrate God who is present in the midst of suffering. These chapters begin the main part of the vision. A door suddenly opens to heaven (4:1). John is invited to enter and see what must take place in the future. By the power of the spirit, he stands before a heavenly throne (4:2), surrounded by twenty-four thrones (4:4) and various creatures and spirits. What follows is less a detailed prediction of future events than an awe-inspiring description of God's worthiness and power, visible "in the spirit" (4:2), but otherwise not seen in the everyday suffering of churches under Roman imperial rule.

John's vision of heaven draws heavily from the Hebrew Scriptures. He was, no doubt, familiar with Job 1—2, for example, which pictures heaven as a royal throne room, with Israel's God, Yahweh, sitting as a monarch, surrounded by heavenly courtiers who execute God's orders. Isaiah 6 also recounts a courtly vision in the Jerusalem temple (6:1). The furniture in the temple's holiest room suddenly springs to life. The cherubim were statues of winged beasts which stood behind the ark of the covenant (Exod. 25:10-22). Yahweh was thought to sit on their outstretched wings. In Isaiah's vision, the cherubim become "seraphim," a pun on the Hebrew word for fire. These now fiery statues come alive, flying back and forth across the room, calling out to one another: "Holy, holy, holy is the Lord of hosts; the whole earth is full of his glory" (6:3). The room fills with smoke and shakes like an earthquake at their call (6:4). "Woe is me!" Isaiah says, "I am lost, for I am a man of unclean lips, and I live among a people of unclean lips; yet my eyes have seen the king, the Lord of hosts!" (6:5).

Nowhere is the heavenly vision more awesome and strange than in the first vision of Ezekiel. Ezekiel had been a priest in the Jerusalem temple, under domination of the Babylonian empire. Israelites mounted a revolt against Babylon, but lost. Then the empire carried Ezekiel and other high-ranking Judean officials into exile in Babylonia (modern-day southern Iraq).

Ezekiel's first vision came in exile. He saw the temple's holiest room coming like a violent storm from the direction of Jerusalem (1:1, 4). The cherubim were now four-faced creatures (1:6), with eyes on every side (1:18). They flew on wheels spinning within wheels (1:16, 19-21), which let them move in any direction without turning around (1:17). Over their heads and outstretched wings was the dome of heaven and, above the dome, a sapphirelike throne, with a brilliant humanlike being, surrounded by rainbow colors as far as the eye could see (1:26-28). Ezekiel's language gets more and more abstract as he moves toward God at the center of the throne:

"This was the appearance of the likeness of the glory of the Lord" (1:28). Words fail. Ezekiel collapses.

Revelation expands the fantastic heavenly visions of Ezekiel and Isaiah. The four-faced winged creatures, full of eyes on every side (a reference to Ezekiel), sing praises to God who sits enthroned (a reference to Isaiah). But in John's vision they sing day and night without ceasing: "Holy, holy, holy, the Lord God the Almighty, who was and is and is to come!" (4:8). Their song adds the dimension of time. Past, present, and future converge in the being of holy, almighty God. Twenty-four elders, possibly representing the twelve tribal ancestors of Israel and the twelve Christian apostles, occupy the twenty-four thrones that flank the throne of God. They cast down their crowns at the feet of God and sing: "You are worthy, our Lord and God, to receive glory and honor and power, for you created all things, and by your will they existed and were created" (4:11). God is worthy of honor and glory throughout creation. Universal praise of God is the lens through which the rest of John's vision appropriately is read.

But ecstatic celebration of God's universal glory does not remove the worshiper from real-world concerns. Revelation's vision of heavenly praise keeps the suffering of persecuted churches prominently displayed. The seven torches, burning constantly before the throne of God (4:5), are seven spirits, corresponding to the seven churches of Asia (1:4) for whom the revelation is given. The "Lamb" who is worthy to open the scroll of the future has seven horns and seven watchful eyes, the seven spirits sent out into the world (5:6).

But the Lamb stands as if it were slaughtered (5:6, 9, 12). This theme of violence and death reminds Christian readers of the violent death of Jesus, but also alludes to the violence befalling the Christian churches of Asia. The image draws on a rich biblical tradition that finds, in the blood of lambs, cleansing from impurity (Lev. 14:10-20) and salvation from death (Exod. 12:3-13, 21-27), themes repeated here in Revelation. The bad news of Jesus' death and the churches' impending persecution is also the good news of the churches' cleansing, salvation, and exaltation to the throne of God.

God holds a scroll (5:1), sealed with seven seals, that contains the script of future events. John weeps bitterly that no one in the universe is found worthy to open the scroll of the future (5:4). Suddenly, next to God's throne, a Lamb appears, representing the

Messiah (5:6). The Lamb alone is worthy to open the scroll of the future.

When the Lamb takes the scroll from the hand of God, all the universe erupts in song—first, those who surround the throne, then the angels, and, finally, every creature in the universe. "You are worthy to take the scroll and to open its seals, for you were slaughtered and by your blood you ransomed for God saints from every tribe and language and people and nation" (5:9). "Worthy is the Lamb who was slaughtered!" (5:12). "Blessing and honor and glory and might forever and ever!" (5:13).

The Lamb neither speaks nor yet opens the scroll of future events. It, rather, holds the future in its hand, prompting universal praise. In these chapters, the emphasis is not on what will happen, but on who holds the future. For us, the revelation has less to do with predicting the future, which only God can know, than with simply embracing God. When the future is cloudy and the present full of pain, hope is found in presence—the presence of a slaughtered Lamb, willing to go with us even through the shadows of death.

Discussion and Action

1. Talk about the Exodus, Isaiah, and Ezekiel images of God's presence. How are they similar to Revelation? What are your first thoughts when you hear each of these Hebrew scriptures? Talk about ways that you feel or see the presence of God.

2. Discuss crisis situations that have been eased by worship or by people "just being present" for the person in crisis.

3. How have members of your group provided a ministry of presence for each other? Discuss ways your group or congregation can carry "ministries of presence" to people in crisis. How are you already doing this? How might you do it better?

4. At which times in your life have you felt you most needed to know the future? How has your need to know changed over the years? What most effectively allays your need to know the future?

5

How Long, O Lord?
Revelation 6:1—8:1

The vision of God's heavenly victory puts the church's earthly suffering in a larger sacred context. Through its worship, the church can experience hope and have a taste of heavenly victory, which gives us strength in the face of frightening circumstances.

Personal Preparation

1. Read the scripture aloud. Chant or sing the parts that are written as direct quotations. Think about how these chapters might be read and sung responsively or otherwise performed during a worship service.
2. Think of a specific time when you felt God's power in the midst of a crisis.
3. Make a list of places where you see evidence of evil, persecution, and injustice this week. Especially look at the newspaper, TV, and magazines for signs of evil in people and events.

Understanding

John's vision gives hope to Christians living in what seem to be hopeless conditions. But in chapters 6—8, the church's deepening crisis itself is actually presented as a sign of hope. This way of thinking may seem curious to those of us who do not face the severe circumstances Christians faced at the end of the first century.

Sometimes, however, it is in the deepest despair that we begin to see hope.

When Christian missionaries first came to the British Isles, they found that December 25 was one of the holiest days of the year for the pagan Celtic people who lived there. That was the day they courageously celebrated the solstice, the year's shortest day and the first day of winter. Courage was necessary because winter was extremely dangerous. People did not have ways to keep food fresh year round. They did the best they could to store the harvest, to protect it from mold, bugs, and other animals. Hunting and fishing supplemented the supply through the winter. Still, many died of starvation during these harsh months.

Yet they celebrated the solstice, the day winter began, because, in the midst of the danger, came the promise of new life. Rather than seeing it as the shortest day of the year, the people celebrated the winter solstice as the rebirth of the sun, the source of earth's fertility. Daylight would last longer each day. The sun's long slide, which began the summer before, screeched to a halt and its ascent began. The fiercest, coldest days lay ahead in January and February. Things would get worse before they got better. Yet the people celebrated, because the sun was reborn and would grow stronger, shine longer every day. Christian missionaries "baptized" this stubbornly hopeful holiday, substituting the Son for the sun and celebrating December 25 as the birth of Christ, the Giver of new life.

Revelation shows a similar kind of hope. There is a "lag time" between the sun's turnaround at solstice and the earth's restored warmth and fertility in spring. For apocalyptic literature like Revelation, there is also a "lag time" between heavenly history and history on earth. If God has just defeated Satan in heaven, then it is only a matter of time before the faithful on earth will see the defeat of the forces of evil.

As in winter, the lag time would see things get much worse for Christians before they got better. Many of the faithful would suffer and perish before the warm light of God would restore life in a new world. But their suffering had a purpose and a glorious end. Christ's revelation to John assured the faithful that their victory was won. So, like expectant parents at the beginning of labor, the faithful could greet their painful and frightening ordeal with joy. Their suffering signaled the birth of the new world.

It is in the context of this hopeful assurance that the frightening imagery of Revelation 6 and 7 must be understood. The cosmic nature of the events described is illustrated by the opening of "seven seals" (6:1). Though Revelation's imagery usually has more than one meaning, the "seven seals" remind the hearer of the seven days of creation, a reminder made most clear in 8:1, in which the opening of the seventh seal prompts complete silence in heaven. As when God stopped work on the seventh day of creation (Gen. 2:1-4a), the opening of the seventh seal causes heaven to stand still. It is a universal sabbath. If the seven days of creation marked the beginning of the world, the opening of the seven seals marks its end.

It is unwise to nail down exact one-to-one correlations between particular symbols in Revelation and specific events, people, and institutions in John's world. Even for the audience in John's time, the rich symbols of the vision had multiple meanings. They spoke to personal, social, religious, and political dimensions of life. But it is important to remember, when we interpret Revelation, that its symbols are firmly rooted in the experience of first-century Asian Christians.

Thus, in the opening of the first seal, when John describes a crowned archer riding a white horse to conquest (6:2), John's audience would have thought of the feared and admired mounted archers of the Parthians, who several decades earlier had defeated the powerful Roman army. When the second rider, mounted on a red horse, takes peace away from the earth, John's audience probably thought of the *Pax Romana*, the "peace of Rome," imposed by the imperial army. Asian Christians were well aware of the anarchy that had swept Judea and other nations who tried unsuccessfully to rebel against Rome. They would have understand well the global chaos that comes when "peace" is removed (6:4). The third rider represents wildly inflated prices for basic foodstuffs, while luxury items were unaffected. It was a familiar pattern to John's contemporaries, who saw the wealthy landowners of their day withhold land from wheat production to plant more lucrative grapes and olives, creating food shortages in the midst of rapidly rising wealth. The fourth rider, Death personified, brings all manner of human destruction (6:8), including military and natural cataclysms known to John's audience, though not on a scale suggested by the vision. The opened fifth seal reveals the souls of faithful martyrs, crying for an end to persecution and judgment against the oppressors. The sixth seal causes the earth to tremble, blots out the sun and moon, and sends shiny stars crashing to earth like fruit stripped from a tree by gale-force winds. Such imagery would have been especially realistic to John's audience who suffered a series of earthquakes in this period and who had recently seen the volcanic cloud of Mt. Vesuvius darken the sky for weeks, blocking the sun's light and blanketing the earth with volcanic ash.

All these images are rooted in, but move far beyond the concrete historical experience of John's audience. Wars, famines, earthquakes, and crop failures take on cosmic dimensions. The natural and social disasters, which swirl together in the ebb and flow of history, are seen as an ever widening, ever more furious eddy, sucking down and swallowing up the kings, generals, and magnates of the earth. The violent images grow out of the Asian churches' experience of a world in upheaval, but they reach far beyond the historical events that gave them rise.

The larger violent scene is really cosmic praise of the all-powerful God who is acting self-sacrificially to save the world. "Salvation belongs to our God who is seated on the throne, and to the Lamb!" the numberless crowd of saints cries (7:10). "Amen! Blessing and glory and wisdom and thanksgiving and honor and power and might be to our God forever and ever!" the angels' song responds (7:12). Universal worship frames all the cataclysms at the world's end.

The cosmic liturgy of praise begins in chapter 7 with the coming together of a universal congregation. The calling of 144,000 saints of Israel is a symbolic heightening of God's magnificent will to save, not a precise, literal figure. By choosing 12,000 saints from each of Israel's 12 tribes, God expresses a boundless intention to save. It is like Jesus' statement (Matt. 18:22) that we should forgive others seventy-seven times. Peter had assumed that forgiving someone seven times pressed the outer limits of generosity. Jesus' response shattered the bounds of human reason, offering unlimited forgiveness instead. So too, the calling of Israel's saints, 12,000 times 12, shows the unlimited scope of God's mercy.

Along with the saints of Israel stands a countless multitude from every nation and every language group, praising God's boundless sovereignty and merciful intention to save (7:9-10). Dressed in white robes, these saints are those who came out of the great end time ordeal, with robes now washed clean, made white by the blood of the Lamb (7:14). It is this purification by Christ, the Lamb, that motivates their worshipful praise (7:15). And it is in the context of this worship that the saints find shelter in God, their Savior (7:15). In their worship, the promise takes on life. "They will hunger no more, and thirst no more; the sun will not strike them, nor any scorching heat; for the Lamb at the center of the throne will be their shepherd, and he will guide them to springs of the water of life, and God will wipe away every tear from their eyes" (7:16-17).

Thus, the vision builds a larger context for the ordeals experienced and expected by the late first-century Christian community. It does not extol suffering. But neither does it belittle the anguish of Christians trying to live faithfully under a political system that claimed divine justification and demanded ultimate allegiance. Nor does the vision promise a way around the suffering of the faithful, whether through miraculous deliverance or through compromise with imperial Rome. Rather, it puts the suffering of the faithful into a cosmic and sacred context. It helps the church find redemption in suffering and strength in the face of frightening circumstances.

It meets head-on the pain of living a faith out of step with the predominant values of the culture and puts that pain in the context of grateful praise for the God who is able and willing to save beyond our wildest imagination. The vision also identifies worship as the place of shelter, where the faithful experience the assurance of salvation in the midst of sometimes violent persecution. In their thankful praise, the faithful are able to see the dawning of a new day. There, they are able to see, through the dark and dangerous days that lie ahead, that life follows death, that victory grows out of defeat, that spring follows winter, that God's radiant power shines stronger, lasts longer, than all the mighty powers that rule the world for yet a little while.

Discussion and Action

1. How do you experience congregational worship as a "place of shelter"? When has worship helped you endure in times of evil or persecution or injustice?

2. How does your weekly worship relate to your everyday life? Is there any part of the worship that usually stays with you during the week? What is it about your worship that makes you feel connected with Christians in other times and places?

3. In nations such as the United States and Canada, where religious liberty is legally protected, what are the things that make Christians "a peculiar people"? What values set Christians apart from the wider society? Is the church too cozy with the "powers that be"?

4. These chapters of Revelation understand everything that happens—personal, political, social, natural, good, and bad—to be part of the cosmic celebration of God's saving power. Is this a good way of looking at it? What are the dangers of such a view? What is positive about this approach to history?

5. Where in the world today is the church giving glory to God through its suffering?

6

Bittersweet Words
Revelation 10:1—11:19

*John receives the bittersweet word of God, which tastes
sweet in the mouth but makes him sick at his stomach.
It is not always easy to discern the truth. Even when we
are confident of what the truth is, speaking it can be very
painful. Yet hope lies in our struggle to discern the truth
and live it boldly.*

Personal Preparation
1. Read chapters 10 and 11 aloud. Chant the heavenly songs
   at the end of chapter 11.
2. Think of trouble spots where Christians face particular
   challenges or danger as they carry out the church's mission.
   Pray specifically for these churches. If you know names of
   particular people in these churches, pray for them by name.
3. Read Ezekiel 2—3 and Daniel 7 as background. How do
   the prophets respond to the visions they see? Do they
   understand them completely? Do they seem comfortable
   with the message they have received?

Understanding
In the early 1960s, a professor at a church-related university in
Mississippi joined many of his colleagues in signing a letter that
called for a nonviolent solution to the controversy over desegre-
gating public schools. He did it out of his Christian conviction.

One evening he and his wife came home to find their babysitter's father sitting in the living room. The babysitter was gone. The couple learned that shortly after they had left someone called the girl and threatened to kill her because she was "a filthy Jew," working for a "nigger-loving communist." The professor was appalled when the girl's father told the story. He apologized to the father and vowed never again to put the man's daughter in that kind of danger.

The father's response stunned him. "No! We cannot give in! Don't change your lifestyle because of these people. If you do, they have won, and none of us are safe. When you want to go out to dinner and a movie, call me. I will babysit. For God's sake, they must not win this! And they won't, if we don't give in!" The unexpected resolve of this mild-mannered neighbor was a sudden burst of hope and courage, an inspiration which strengthened the professor in the difficult days ahead.

Speaking and acting out of one's faith commitment is not always easy. It is hard enough, sometimes, just to know what is right in difficult situations. Even when the correct course of action is clear, it may carry a high price. Words as sweet as Isaiah 56:7, "my house will be called a house of prayer for all people," can be a bitter threat when people are divided by race, religion, lifestyle, or nationality. Simple acts of acceptance become signs of judgment against those who want to exclude. Sweet words of acceptance from those who love, offered to the oppressed, may anger and enrage those who hate, endangering everybody.

In his heavenly vision John received a bittersweet message from God. Chapter 10 begins an interlude between the sixth and seventh trumpets, which the angels of heaven blow to announce a series of natural disasters about to come as judgment against the wicked (see 8:6). The interlude (10:1—11:14) begins with a giant angel coming down to earth, setting one foot on the land and the other on the sea (10:1-2). Grasping a little scroll (10:2), the angel gives a great shout. His voice roars like a lion and prompts seven loud crashes of thunder (10:3), which carry some sort of message. But when John starts to write what the thunders had said, a heavenly voice stops him (10:4). Even in the most direct of messages from God, some things remain hidden to us. Our knowledge is incomplete. "We know only in part, and we prophesy only in part . . . we see in a mirror, dimly" (1 Cor. 13:9, 12).

Even when God's will is clear to us, it is not always easy to swallow. John is instructed to take the scroll now open in the angel's hand (10:8) and eat it (10:9). True to the angel's prediction, the scroll tastes sweet in John's mouth, but makes him sick at his stomach (10:9-10). The pleasant words of God become bitterness for the prophet who now must prophesy against many peoples and powerful rulers (10:11).

The bittersweet scroll of Revelation 10:8-11 stands in a long tradition of Hebrew prophecy. Ezekiel describes God's word as a scroll, which tastes sweet as honey when the prophet eats it (2:8—3:3). Jeremiah talks about God's words as something to eat with joy (15:16). But in both of these cases, the delightful taste of God's prophetic word brings suffering to the one prophet who must declare that word. Jeremiah complains to God, "Know that on your account I suffer insult" (Jer. 15:15). God warns Ezekiel that he will live in danger because of the prophecy: "I send you . . . to a nation of rebels . . . . do not be afraid of them, and do not be afraid of their words, though briers and thorns surround you and you live among scorpions" (Ezek. 2:3, 6). So too, the apocalyptic visionary Daniel feels the pain of his prophetic knowledge: "My spirit was troubled within me and the visions of my head terrified me" (7:15). "Because of the vision, such pains have come upon me that I retain no strength. How can [I] talk with my Lord? For I am shaking, no strength remains in me, and no breath is left in me" (Dan. 10:16-17).

Knowing the truth and doing the right thing can be painful. A doctor in a small community became convinced that chemical pollution from the plant just outside of town was poisoning the water and air. The cancer rates in that area had risen steadily the last few years and now were substantially higher than regional averages. More and more frequently, the doctor found traces of a cancer-causing compound in blood samples, a compound produced as a by-product of one of the industrial processes in the plant. The plant employed about half of the town's work force in relatively well-paying jobs. Another 40 percent were employed in stores, shops, restaurants, and schools that serviced the plant and its employees. If the plant closed, most of the townspeople would lose their jobs. The doctor took the data she collected to the plant management, who rejected her findings and warned her that any further meddling would jeopardize the economic viability of the company. But she knew that if she kept quiet, her neighbors would likely develop cancer and the land and water might be poisoned for many years to come. If she went public with the information, the plant might close and the town might die. The truth sometimes carries a high personal price for those who bear it, as well as those who hear it.

John's bittersweet revelation would carry a high price for those who tell the truth. At the beginning of chapter 11, Jesus authorizes two "witnesses" to prophesy for a period of three and a half years (11:3). In Greek, this word "witness" is *martyrs*, the root of the English word *martyr*. Elsewhere in Revelation, it is used only to describe the crucified and risen Jesus (1:5; 3:14) and Antipas, a Christian "witness" in Pergamum who was killed for his faith (2:13). Like Moses and Aaron just before the exodus from Egypt (Exod. 7—12), these two witnesses are authorized to bring drought and plagues (11:5-6) against their foes. Once their testimony is finished, however, the witnesses will be killed by a monster that emerges from the bottomless pit (11:7) and leaves their dead bodies lying in a Jerusalem street (11:8). A general celebration of their death will come to a sudden halt at the end of three and a half days, when the breath of God enters their corpses and they stand on their feet, terrifying all who see them (11:10-11). At an invitation from heaven, they will rise in a cloud, prompting an earthquake that will destroy a tenth of the city and 7000 people (11:12-13) before it is all over. The witnesses who proclaim the prophetic word and the people against whom it is spoken all suffer because of it.

Chapter 11 concludes with the sounding of the seventh trumpet. But unlike earlier trumpets, the seventh does not result in planetary disaster. Rather, it prompts a universal chorus of praise for the beginning of the messianic kingdom. The final rage of the nations has now been spent. God Almighty has taken power and, with the Messiah, has begun to reign (11:16-17). God's heavenly temple is opened (11:19), and the faithful servants, the prophets and saints who fear and serve God, are rewarded (11:18). On the other side of their suffering and death, God's universal reign begins. In the end, it is that universal reign that makes sense of the suffering.

The word of truth sometimes comes at a heavy price. It is hard enough to know the right thing to do in many of the circumstances we confront. We see in part and prophesy in part. But even when our Christian convictions lead us to a clear course of action, there often is a price to pay, a pain to bear. Truth does not come cheap. But out of the struggle to offer a faithful witness can come a sudden burst of hope, an inspired confidence in the reign of God brought a little bit closer by each courageous act of truth.

Discussion and Action

1. Recap some of your Bible reading. What was bittersweet in the Ezekiel and Daniel texts? What is bittersweet in John's message?

2. Discuss times when you have had to say something or do something difficult but right.

3. Think of times when Christian words of love, acceptance, and peace prompted a bitter reaction? How did the church respond to the reaction? How should it respond?

4. Name some issues confronting the church today that we "see in a mirror, dimly"—issues that leave us uncertain about what the church should be doing. What makes them so difficult to figure out? How can we have a clearer understanding of them?

5. Get the names and addresses of missionaries or service workers your church supports. Lift them up in prayer. Write them to let them know of your love and support. Invite them to visit your congregation when possible.

7

In the Clutches of the Beast
Revelation 12:1-12; 13:1-18

Rome and its apologists are symbolized as "dragon and beast." For a while yet the awesome power of the imperial economic, political, and cultural system is invincible on earth, at least for a short while yet. Christians always live constrained by such powerful systems, networks of good and evil that are beyond the power of individual people to control. Though implicated in the evil of the systems, Christians must hold up the vision of "systemic good," the dominion of God.

Personal Preparation

1. Read the scriptures and think about their meaning in the first century.
2. Fast one day if your health permits (or do a partial fast, drinking water and juice from sunup to sundown). On that day pray for those people in the world who do not have access to adequate food, clothing, shelter, or health care.
3. Think of some of the systemic evils in your community, state, province, or nation, such as poverty, homelessness, and racism. What is your responsibility as a Christian toward such evil?
4. Read materials from your church's mission agencies about economic conditions in some of the places where you support missions.

Understanding

Throughout the vast banana plantations of central Jamaica are signs warning people not to drink the water. Water and land are toxic there because of the pesticides and herbicides that keep bananas plentiful and cheap for export. Other signs warn: No Trespassing! Animals Will Be Impounded. Humans Will Be Shot! With chicken and fish costing the equivalent of two weeks' pay, people there are tempted to grab a bunch of bananas when nobody is looking. But if very many Jamaicans are allowed to steal bananas, the supply will go down, the price will go up, and Jamaican bananas will not be able to compete with Costa Rican bananas for the business of North American supermarkets. Jamaican banana pickers will lose their jobs. The people who spray the poison and put up the No Trespassing signs are not necessarily cruel, uncaring people. They are simply following the logic of the economic system they have inherited. Given the way the system works, they are doing the best they can.

The great Catholic theologian Karl Rahner described the doctrine of "original sin," by using the example of buying a banana. "[W]hen someone buys a banana, he does not reflect upon the fact that its price is tied to many presuppositions. To them belongs, under certain circumstances, the pitiful lot of banana pickers, which in turn is co-determined by social injustice, exploitation, or a centuries-old commercial policy. The person himself now participates in this situation of guilt to his own advantage. Where does this person's personal responsibility in taking advantage of such a situation . . . end, and where does it begin?" (*Foundations of Christian Faith* 110-111). For Jamaican land and water not to be poisoned and trespassers not to be shot, the supply of bananas most likely would have to go down and their price up.

Indirectly, I participate in sin against the Jamaican people every time I buy a cheap bunch of bananas. Perhaps I could buy grapes or oranges instead, but what does that solve? Maybe I could wash my hands of the whole affair, move off into the woods and grow my own. But then I would abdicate my Christian responsibility to make a difference in the world. Whichever way I turn, I sin. I want to do the right thing, but the system leaves me no choice but to do that which is wrong. "I do not do the good I want, but the evil I do not want is what I do" (Rom. 7:19). This is the nature of "systemic evil." It is greater than individual people and, to a large extent, beyond their individual power to control. Systemic evil calls for collective action.

Revelation 12—13 addresses the problem of systemic evil and holds out hope that good can still come from earthly systems. This section begins with a heavenly woman clothed with sun and moon and wearing a twelve-star crown. She is in the final stage of labor, about to give birth to a son who would rule the world (12:5). The son, described in messianic terms (cf. Ps. 2), is Jesus. The woman may be Israel, but later appears to be the persecuted church. Just as she is about to deliver, a great red dragon appears in heaven, with ten horns and seven crowns on its seven heads (12:3; cf. Dan. 7). It crouches before the woman, ready to eat the child as soon as it is born (12:4). But the child is whisked away to God, and the woman flees to a safe haven in the wilderness. The angels of God (cf. Dan. 10) begin to battle the dragon and its angels. The dragon is defeated and cast out of heaven, and its true identity is revealed: it is the devil, Satan.

The good news is that the devil is defeated in heaven. The bad news is that Satan is now set loose on earth. "Rejoice then, you heavens and those who dwell in them! But woe to the earth and the sea, for the devil has come down to you with great wrath, because he knows that his time is short!" (12:12). The church's earthly suffering is a sign of Satan's heavenly defeat. Its faithfulness in persecution is the power by which Satan falls: "They have conquered him by the blood of the Lamb and by the word of their testimony, for they did not cling to life even in the face of death" (12:11). In the end, the church's perseverance defeats Satan.

The dragon unsuccessfully pursues the heavenly mother (12:12-18) and then turns to make war on her children, those who keep the testimony (*martyria*) of Jesus (12:17). As the dragon takes a stand on the seashore (12:18), a beast rises up out of the sea (13:1), followed later by a land monster (13:11).

The description of the dragon and the two beasts reminds us of Daniel 7 and draws heavily from ancient Near Eastern myths about primordial serpents of chaos who had to be defeated in order for the world to be created (compare Job 7:12; 26:12-13; Pss. 74:12-15; 89:10-11; Isa. 51:9-10; 2 Esd. 6:49-52). The appearance of the dragon and the beasts on earth represents the undoing of the universe, a return to the chaotic "formless void" that preceded creation (Gen 1:1-2). Their ultimate defeat will signal the creation of a new world.

The first beast (13:1-2) is a composite of the four sea beasts of Daniel 7. It resembles a leopard (Dan. 7:6), a bear (Dan. 7:5) and a lion (Dan. 7:4), with seven heads bearing ten crowned horns (Dan. 7:7). Elsewhere in Revelation, the seven heads of the beast are said to be "seven mountains" (as well as seven kings [17:9]), on which the imperial capital, referred to as "Babylon," sits. (Rome, the imperial capital of John's world, was built on seven hills.) When John says that one of the beast's heads received a death blow from a sword, yet survived (13:3, 12, 14), he was referring to the evil anti-Christian Caesar, Nero. Nero had committed suicide by sinking a dagger into his neck. Much like Elvis sightings and Hitler legends, a popular superstition soon took hold across the Roman empire that Nero either had not actually died or else had come back to life and was about to resume power with a terrible vengeance. The beast was arrogant and mouthy, constantly boasting and blaspheming God (13:5-6; cf. Dan. 7:8, 11; 11:36-37). In a transparent reference to Roman emperor worship, John records that all the earth followed the beast and worshiped it and the dragon Satan who gave it authority (13:3-4).

After warning the saints of their impending captivity and martyrdom and exhorting them to remain faithful under the onslaught of the beast, John describes a second monster. This two-horned beast rises out of the earth and makes the whole world worship the first beast. It performs signs and miracles that deceive people into worshiping an idol of the beast. This may refer to the "false teachers" inside the church, whom John condemns for teaching that Christians can participate in the emperor cult. But it may also refer to the imperial priests who used fire and light tricks and ventriloquism to dupe the populace (Boring 157). The beast causes the execution of those who refuse to worship the idol (13:15). This may refer to threats used to get information about Christians (2:9-10) or to the Roman officials who enforced emperor worship. The beast could mark all people and control all economic activity, a power reserved for the empire. Those who do not bear the mark of the beast—for example, Christians who violate the emperor cult—can be cut out of the economic system with disastrous personal consequences.

Finally, John identifies the beast by Hebrew numerology: "Let anyone with understanding calculate the number of the beast, for it is the number of a person. Its number is six hundred sixty-six" (13:18). In Jewish apocalyptic thought, 7 symbolized perfect wholeness—the joining of heaven (symbolized by the number 3) and earth (symbolized as 4). In this number game, 6 just misses the mark. It falls short of perfection. Since heaven is symbolized by the number 3, three 6s represent imperfection in divine proportions. But John is not just speaking generally about imperfection. The number 666 also refers to a specific person, he says. John already has alluded to the Nero legend (13:3, 12, 14). And, using the numerical equivalents of the Hebrew alphabet (each letter is assigned a numerical value), the letters of "Neron Caesar" equal 666. The extra *n* at the end of "Nero" also appears in the Dead Sea Scrolls. The numerical total without the extra *n* is 616, the number that appears instead of 666 in other ancient texts of Revelation. John at least had Nero in mind, but the symbol of the beast refers to much more than an individual emperor. It is the whole system Nero represents.

The beast is that evil that goes far beyond individual sin, those bad thoughts and unkind actions which stain our personal morality. Much more sinister than that, the beast is the evil of political, economic, and cultural systems, which individuals acting alone may be virtually powerless to change (13:7).

Several years ago, Christians became concerned about the impact of infant formula sales in countries, particularly in Africa, where unsafe supplies of drinking water made the formula ineffective at best. European and North American companies were marketing their products by giving free samples to hospitals and clinics there, using the health care system to encourage women to substitute infant formula for breastmilk. This strategy became especially problematic when families ran out of free samples. By then they were dependent on the formula and convinced that formula feeding was superior to breastfeeding, but they lacked the money to purchase an adequate amount. So vast numbers of mothers tried to stretch their supplies by diluting the formula with water—water filled with bacteria and amoebas that caused a number of infants to become very sick, often fatally ill. The economic forces that led to such widespread personal tragedy seemed insurmountable, and the infant formula companies showed no readiness to change.

To address this systemic problem, Christians in North America and Europe spearheaded an international boycott of all products made by one of the infant formula companies, Nestle. The Nestle boycott, which lasted for years, finally won the company's agreement to end its destructive marketing practices in Africa and elsewhere. By the perseverance and collective action of Christians around the world, a systemic evil was met and conquered. Countless individuals, acting together in choosing not to buy a candy bar, altered the direction of a powerful economic force and thereby offered life to countless individuals half a world away.

In the face of powerful systemic evil, our hope is in the vision of "systemic good" held out by those who bear the testimony of God's perfect dominion, where life is abundant and all things are made healthy and whole. By faithful perseverance and working together, that ancient serpent, the deceiver of the world, is conquered. Its poison no longer pollutes. And the children of the heavenly mother, now free, can eat the food of heaven and drink the pure water of life eternal.

Discussion and Action

1. Review the imagery used in the scriptures for this session. What did the symbols mean to John's early readers. What do they mean for Christians today?

2. Have you ever been caught in a bind at work where "the good of the company" (greater efficiency, better profitability, more competitiveness) led to unfair suffering for individuals (layoffs, paycuts, demotions)? If you made or implemented the decision, how did you come to terms with it? If you were one who suffered, who, if anyone, did you blame? In either case, how could you as an individual have changed what happened?

3. Tell personal stories about bad experiences with highly bureaucratic, heavily computerized companies or government agencies. Was it easy to get the problem straightened out? Which individual person was responsible for the foul-up? Did you yell at anybody? Was it that person's fault? Is there something about the "system" that makes this kind of problem occur? Could such problems be avoided if individuals would just do better?

4. Identify some "systems" that affect your life, for good or for bad. As a Christian, how can you maintain a strong witness for wholeness in the face of these powerful and imperfect systems?
5. If you could make the world over to be the kind of place it ought to be, what would it be like? How would it be different from the way it is now? How would it be the same? What would *you* do differently? How might we begin to move toward that kind of world?

8

God Is Victorious
Revelation 14:1-7; 18:1—19:10

"Babylon" (the imperial power of Rome) falls. This vision of Rome's defeat comes not as Rome is on its last legs, but at the very height of Roman power. Systemic evil seems invincible, but even the most powerful systems eventually unravel. Christians caught in the web of systemic evil must respond not with resigned despair, but with repentant hope for the new world fast approaching.

Personal Preparation

1. Read all of chapters 14 through 19, and then reread the text for this session.
2. Scan the book of Nahum to see how a Hebrew prophet responded to the fall of one of Israel's imperial oppressors. Does anything about this book make you uncomfortable?
3. Think about times when something you thought impossible really happened.
4. Check labels and owner's manuals of some of the things you own to find out where they were made. Do you know anything about the governments there? working conditions? average wages? environmental protection? If working people there made about the same money as working people here, could we afford to own all the things we own?

Understanding

On Ash Wednesday, 1980, a group of us went down to New York City to conduct a peaceful protest at a "think tank" that planned strategies for global thermonuclear war. As I stood chatting with the captain of the police who had come to make sure nothing would get out of hand, a television reporter asked me why we were there. "We are Christians," I said. "This is Ash Wednesday, a day of repentance. We have come to this place where plans are made for the destruction of whole populations and maybe even the end of life on this planet. We come here to repent of the things we do as individuals and as a nation that make the things they plan inside this building seem reasonable and necessary."

Later in the day, as we started to leave, the police captain told me, "I hope the world listens to what you people are saying! I hope we get what you're working for." The joy I felt at his surprising word of support still couldn't quiet this nagging feeling I had that the cold war system was simply too powerful to be overcome. Its crazy logic of "mutually assured destruction" seemed impenetrable, particularly since there was an extremely repressive regime in power in the Soviet Union and there were so many economic interests at stake on both sides.

A little over a decade later, I was airport-hopping the morning after the president of the United States and the president of the Russian Republic signed a treaty scrapping two-thirds of the world's nuclear arsenal. I was astonished that newspapers across the country ran the nuclear treaty as their second story, on the bottom of the front page! The indictment of a former White House official was deemed more important news. By that time, the Soviet Union had already collapsed. The United States and Russia had stopped pointing their nuclear weapons at each other and had gone off of full alert. The world had changed dramatically since Ash Wednesday, 1980. What that police captain and I thought was an unlikely dream was now so commonplace as to get second billing in the nation's newspapers. In just over a decade, the impossible became the expected.

Systems of evil often are so powerful that they seem invincible. Holding faithfully to an alternative vision of the way the world should be may seem ridiculous and futile. But even the most powerful of systems can unravel. And once they start to crumble, they often crash with lightning speed.

Chapters 14 through 19 of Revelation describe the crumbling of the powerful system that oppressed first-century churches. This section begins with the Lamb standing on Mount Zion (14:1), the hill where the Jerusalem temple had stood. Along with him were 144,000 people on whose foreheads were written the names of the Lamb and its Father. This heavenly multitude sang a new song which only they knew how to sing (14:3).

The curious remark that these are the people "who have not defiled themselves with women, for they are virgins" (14:4) is clarified somewhat in the next verse: "In their mouth no lie was found: they are blameless" (14:5). Remember that the letters to the seven churches of Asia (chaps. 2—3) are particularly concerned about "false teachers" who deceive the church by saying that Christians can pay homage to the deified emperor without violating their Christian faith. John describes participation in this emperor cult as "fornication" and compares at least one of these "false teachers" to an adulterer who tempts the innocent to "fornicate" (2:14, 20-22). The 144,000 "virgins" are those who resist emperor worship.

Suddenly, an angel flies across heaven proclaiming "an eternal gospel" to the entire world (14:6): "Fear God and give him glory, for the hour of his judgment has come; and worship him who made heaven and earth, the sea and springs of water" (14:7). Throughout Revelation to this point, the faithful have been warned about the insurmountable power of the Roman Empire and its agents and apologists. The "beast" would conquer God's prophets and kill them (11:7). It would capture and kill God's faithful (13:10) and wreak havoc on earth (12:12-17). But now comes the hour of judgment: "Fallen, fallen is Babylon the great!" an angel cries out in a mighty voice (18:2). The power of Rome is crushed. The invincible empire suddenly crumbles.

It is noteworthy that John writes this vision at the height of Roman power. In John's day there was no more realistic hope that Rome would fall than there was a chance in 1980 that the Cold War would collapse. The celebration of "Babylon's" fall is not after-the-fact gloating. It is risky prediction which, at best, would have met with ridicule and, at worst, would have put John and his Christian supporters in danger for treason.

John's thinly veiled description of Rome as "Babylon . . . the whore" (17:5) is not intended as a secret code to hide the true meaning from Roman authorities. John already had been exiled because of "the testimony of Jesus" (1:9), so he apparently was not afraid of Roman authority. Besides, John's description of Rome as "Babylon, the whore" is completely transparent. The whore sat on seven mountains (17:9), just as Rome sits on seven hills. She was "the great city that rules over the kings of the earth" (17:18), "the mighty city" (18:10), "clothed in fine linen, in purple and scarlet, adorned with gold, with jewels, and with pearls" (18:16). "All who had ships at sea grew rich by her wealth" (18:19). She was the center of world trade, whose "merchants were the magnates of the earth" (18:23). Anyone reading Revelation in the late first century would have recognized that "Babylon" was Rome.

So why didn't John just say "Rome" when he meant Rome? Perhaps, he spoke of "Babylon" because he understood that the systemic evil of Roman imperialism was not limited to Rome. It was, rather, an ancient evil, with a long history and a series of incarnations. In Israel's history, systemic evil was embodied in Egyptian, Assyrian, Babylonian, Persian, Greek, Ptolemaic, Seleucid, and finally Roman imperial rule. Among all these, "Babylon" is particularly apt as a symbol of destructive imperial power, because the Babylonians destroyed Jerusalem and its temple and exiled the Jewish people (586 B.C.). Centuries later, after the temple was rebuilt, the Romans also sacked the holy site (A.D. 70) and so were associated with Babylonians in the popular mind. By describing the evil power of Roman imperialism as "Babylon," John calls the ancient and modern reader to understand that systemic evil stretches across time and space and takes on an endless variety of faces.

Evil made many appearances before the Roman empire came onto the historical scene, but its manifestation in the glorious city of Rome would be its last, according to Revelation. Immediately after the long celebration and lament for "Babylon's" demise (Rev. 18), heaven erupts in songs of victory: "Hallelujah! Salvation and glory and power to our God, for his judgments are true and just; he has judged the great whore who corrupted the earth with her fornication, and he has avenged on her the blood of his servants. . . . Hallelujah! The smoke goes up from her forever and ever. . . . Hallelujah! For the Lord our God the Almighty reigns. Let us rejoice . . . for the marriage of the Lamb has come" (19:1-3, 6-7). The fall of Rome would signal the final victory of God, the end of history as we know it and the beginning of the messianic age, the new world, the dominion of God.

We are reading Revelation centuries after the Roman empire disintegrated, and we know that the glory of Rome turned out not to be evil's swan song. Evil has been plentiful ever since the days of the empire. Despite great hopes, the messianic age did not come as quickly as the original readers of Revelation had reason to expect (22:20). So we who read Revelation nineteen centuries later face an important question: What is God saying to us through this text?

If, in Revelation, "Babylon" refers to the systemic evils that underlie all oppressive empires up to and including Rome, then "Babylon" also may describe the systemic evil of empires that came after Rome. In our own century, we might think of Nazi fascism or Stalinist communism as particularly virulent examples of the systemic evil described in the pages of Revelation.

But the description of "Babylon," in all its economic glory and power, suggests that Christians in the United States and Canada also must look closer to home. "The merchants of the earth have grown rich from the power of her luxury" (18:3). "She glorified herself and lived luxuriously" (18:7)—well fed (18:14), well dressed (18:16), with ready access to high culture (18:22). An economic superpower, "Babylon" imported and exported all manner of goods and services (18:13-17). Wealth flowed to it from other nations. Its business leaders were the "magnates of the earth" (18:23). It sat at the top of the world economy, rewarding those governments who danced to its tune (18:3, 9, 23) and punishing those who did not (18:24). Not surprisingly, "Babylon" considered itself the greatest nation on earth, a superpower who would never suffer defeat (18:7).

The systemic evil of Babylon is not only "back then" or "over there." It is also right here among us whose nation sits at the top of the world's economic ladder—among us who, with powerful social sanction, have developed an insatiable appetite for consumer goods. Like ancient Rome, North Americans own an astonishingly high percentage of the world's wealth, though we constitute a very small percentage of its population. Our feverish consumption fuels this global inequity and, in the process, fouls the air, water, and land. In the words of the comic strip "Pogo" at the height of the Watergate scandal, "We have met the enemy and it is us!"

To be sure, Babylon-like evil is found all over the globe, wherever the powerful dominate the weak. Christians must provide a strong witness against such malevolent power wherever it rears its head. But for North American Christians, confronting Babylon especially means confronting ourselves, confronting our obsession with consumer goods, our frenzy to work more so we can buy more, our never ending push to live just one step beyond our means. For us, confronting Babylon means personal repentance, daily decisions to turn our backs on the endless overwork and consumption to which our society is addicted. It means resting, buying less, giving more, committing ourselves increasingly to "live simply so others might simply live."

Sing the songs of God's victory over Babylon. As you sing, weep; for we are Babylon, caught in a web of systemic evil too strong for us alone to break. But remember that even the most powerful systems are not eternal. They can unravel with lightning speed. Empires fall. Cold wars collapse. In the blinking of an eye, the impossible becomes the commonplace. In such a world, the faithful respond to powerful systems of evil not with resigned despair, but with repentant hope. They see new visions, sing new songs of a new world fast approaching.

Discussion and Action

1. Read Mary's Magnificat (Luke 1:46-55). How does this relate to Revelation 18—19? Do these passages strike you as good news or bad news? What, if anything, makes you uncomfortable with their message?
2. Respond to the author's notion that as we sing about God's victory over Babylon, we need also to weep, for we are Babylon. In what ways are we like Babylon?
3. If self-glorification, luxurious living, and ruling by violence are a big part of what makes Babylon sinful (18:7), then what would it mean for us to repent? What is the testimony of Jesus in our world today?
4. Talk about the issues raised in Personal Preparation question 4. How do you respond to those questions?
5. How should the world be different than it is? What is needed to make it different?

9

Judgment at the Mercy Seat
Revelation 20:11—22:5

In the vision of the final judgment and New Jerusalem, there is a tension between judgment and mercy, between our evil works and God's unending grace. Clear lines are drawn between holy and unholy, yet God invites all the nations into the holy city for healing. In the here and now, we also live in a constant tension between judgment and mercy. The challenge for Christians is to uphold a vision that offers neither "cheap grace" nor "just retribution," but offers us forgiveness at the same time it holds us accountable.

Personal Preparation

1. Read Revelation 20:11—22:5 aloud during the week, paying attention to the themes of justice and mercy.
2. Think of times you expected to be punished but were surprised by mercy. When have you experienced God's mercy?
3. Listen to a recording of "The Holy City" for meditation.
4. Read the words of the hymn "Beyond a Dying Sun" (p. 83).

Understanding

After the fall of the Somoza dictatorship in Nicaragua in 1979, several of the dreaded National Guardsmen were arrested and tried for human rights violations. One such man was brought before

Tomás Borge, a revolutionary leader who became a cabinet minister in the new government. The guardsman had overseen and participated in the severe torture of Borge and the torture and execution of his wife. Borge now had the power of life and death over his enemy. "What is his punishment, Commandante?" they asked. Borge looked the man in the eye and said, "Your punishment is this: I forgive you."

Often we are caught between mercy and justice. We have a deep-seated conviction that the guilty must pay for their crime, yet we realize that they don't always. It is no accident that the surefire theater blockbusters are the action hero movies, where criminals are plain evil and justice is executed with great speed and violence, cutting the cumbersome red tape of due process. These movies tap a deep root in us that says there is, or at least there ought to be, a cosmic law where good deeds are rewarded and bad deeds punished. In this life, at least, that cosmic law doesn't seem to operate all that well. The righteous all too often suffer and the wicked prosper. The legal system often seems to work better for the criminals than it does for the victims. So, in our movies and television shows, we live out the just world we wish we had, where clever detectives and lawyers crack the case and good guys blow away bad guys.

But even as guns blaze and audiences cheer, we cannot help but worry about the real world effect of this fantasy-world street justice. Ours is a violent society. Swift and violent "justice" is meted out every day on city streets between warring gangs; in homes between husbands and wives, parents and children; and in the world between races, cultures, and nations. Often the violence is cyclical; one violent deed begets another in retaliation, which begets yet another and on and on. The cycle is perpetuated out of our deep sense of justice—the guilty must pay. But when our sense of justice demands retaliation, the cycle of retribution continues. With each round, the stakes get higher and the violence grows.

In addition to the problem of stopping the violence, we also face the difficulty of figuring out where it began and who to blame. In our social and political life, we often encounter the same thing parents frequently face trying to figure out a just solution to a sibling fight. Maybe it started with "Don't touch me!" followed shortly by an "accidental" brush. "I just barely touched her! She didn't have to punch me!" "Well, he stuck his tongue out at me!" "She made a face at me!" And so on *ad infinitum*. When there is a history of mistrust, it is hard to determine who started it, which act of violence is just retribution, and which is outright provocation.

Furthermore, bad deeds don't just spring out of nowhere. Psychologists tell us that criminals are made, not born. Often abusers were themselves abused. Many brutal adults were brutalized children. Poverty breeds hopelessness and hopelessness, violence. Social and psychological abuse often predisposes the victim to lash out later at others.

As long as we view wrongdoers one-dimensionally and see their criminal acts as isolated events unconnected to any other events, we can easily work up a feeling of revenge—eye for eye, tooth for tooth, life for life. But when we look at them as human beings with personal stories of love, hope, promise, ridicule, deprivation, and disappointment, it is difficult to escape twinges of sorrow and compassion and mixed feelings of anger and mercy.

It is, of course, unhealthy to suppress the rage we feel at being victimized or seeing others victimized by violent people. And likewise, a shallow mercy that holds no one responsible and tries to sweep a victim's pain under the rug serves only to perpetuate the injustice. "Cheap grace," like street justice, never solves the injustice; it merely disguises it or covers it up. Ultimately, justice without mercy, retribution without grace, spirals out of control and destroys everything and everyone in its path. To escape violence at all, mercy and justice must be held together.

The final chapters of John's vision demonstrate this kind of tension between judgment and grace in the heavenly realm, the same balance we need here and now. Today's scripture begins with a heavenly courtroom scene where roles are reversed. Instead of Christians on trial for refusing to worship Caesar, all the resurrected dead are waiting to be judged according to their works (20:12). Several books are opened in the courtroom (20:12), including "the book of life" (cf. 3:5; 13:8; 17:8). Earlier, the book of life is said to contain names "written . . . from the foundation of the world" (13:8; 17:8), hinting at some kind of "predestination" or, at least, "foreknowledge" of those who would be spared at the great judgment. Whatever hint of predestination there may be in all of this, however, is balanced by the presence of other books that record the deeds of all the resurrected and form a judgment only after all the evidence is in. In the end, however, those who are thrown into the "lake of fire" (20:15) are those whose names are not written from the beginning of the world in the book of life. Subsequent generations of Christians would fight and divide over rigid distinctions between predestination and free will. John's vision embraces both.

In chapter 21, John describes "a new heaven and a new earth." A "new Jerusalem . . . prepared as a bride adorned for her husband" (21:2; cf. 3:12) descends from heaven. God and humans will share a new intimacy, never before experienced. God's "home" will be among humans and God will "dwell" with them as their God (21:3). In the Greek, *home* and *dwell* are, at root, the same word. Basically, it means "tent" or "tabernacle" (cf. Exod. 26; 36; 40; Num. 1; 3; 9). In the Hebrew Scriptures, it is the place where God lived before the Jerusalem temple was built. From now on, John reports, God will "tabernacle" with the people. That is, God will pitch a tent with them, live where they live, go where they go. John sees no temple in New Jerusalem, because the people are God's dwelling place. God with us is our holy place. The whole renewed universe is filled with God's presence. The new world is God's temple.

Even though God is with us, we still experience judgment as well as mercy. Along with God's universal presence comes universal purity that judges and rejects anything that is not pure. "Nothing unclean will enter it, nor anyone who practices abomination or falsehood" (21:27). "Those who conquer" are heirs of the new world (21:7), faithful Christians who resist the temptations of idol worship, whose endurance in the face of persecution leads to purity. Those are excluded who are "cowardly" in the face of persecution, "polluted" with the "fornication" of idolatry, whose lies lead others down the same "adulterous" path (21:8; cf. 2:14, 20-23). These are the enemies of the church, within and without, who coerce and tempt the faithful to compromise with imperial culture. Their place is the "lake that burns with fire" (21:8). The very holiness of New Jerusalem implies judgment against the unholy.

Yet, the portrait of New Jerusalem also implies the gracious healing of the impure, despite their own unworthiness. Those who inherit the new world are regenerated by an undeserved, gracious gift of God. "See, I am making all things new," says the one seated on the throne (21:5). God will "wipe every tear from their eyes. Death will be no more; mourning and crying and pain will be no more, for the first things have passed away" (21:4). By a slight modification of Jeremiah 31:33, Revelation makes a significant point. God reveals to Jeremiah that in a renewed Israel "I will be their God, and they shall be my people." Revelation makes "people" plural ("they will be his peoples" [21:3]), expanding the scope of those included. The Jeremiah passage goes on to envision a world in which God "will forgive their iniquity, and remember their sin no more" (Jer. 31:34). Revelation also envisions a world no longer stained by its own impurity and thus separated from God.

Especially striking is the promise that "the nations will walk" by the light of the Lamb, "and the kings of the earth will bring their glory into it" (21:24). Earlier in the book, nations and kings were impure to say the least. "All the nations" have drunk the wine of Babylon's fornication, and "the kings of the earth have committed fornication with her" (18:3). Perhaps the surprising appearance of these fornicating "nations" and "kings of the earth" in New Jerusalem is best explained by the "tree of life" (cf. Gen. 2:9; 3:22-24) that grows in the city's center (22:2). Its leaves are for healing the nations (22:2), so that nothing cursed will any longer be found there (22:3). It is perhaps the healing power of New Jerusalem that may explain why the gates of a walled city such as Jerusalem are always open (21:25). All nations enter (21:24, 26), but no one ever leaves.

Justice and mercy. Judgment and grace. In the completed work of the Alpha and Omega, these are held together. Like a light flipped on at dusk, the light of the Lamb in New Jerusalem suddenly makes boundaries clear. Just moments before, everything was shadowy and gray, but now, inside New Jerusalem, colors spring to life, contrasting with the pitch darkness on the outside. Here in this new place God is judgmental and merciful, but God's judgment draws the convicted toward the light of mercy. The gates of New Jerusalem are open as long as it's daylight. And there is no night there. All are welcome. Clean and unclean, saint and sinner, nations and kings and subject peoples. All are invited to come and be healed. Our merciful judging God wonderfully sentences us, pardons us, and gives us our example: "Your punishment is this: I forgive you."

Discussion and Action

1. Quickly glance through the scripture and summarize the action in the order that it happened. Also, list the many symbols and images, such as the great white throne, the book of life, lake of fire, and the New Jerusalem.

2. Talk about God's world made new. What roles do mercy and justice play? Are there things we can do in the here and now to make at least part of that new world a reality?
3. Tell about a time when you found yourself torn between mercy and punishment? How did you resolve this?
4. Has your church ever experienced a cycle of verbal violence, where warring factions seemed trapped in endless retaliation? How can such a cycle of violence and retaliation be broken or avoided? How might judgment and mercy be brought to bear in such situations?
5. Discuss other situations where people are caught in cycles of violent retribution. How might those cycles be broken?
6. Discuss the idea that "God's judgment draws the converted toward the light of mercy. . . . all are welcome. . . . all are invited to come and be healed."
7. Listen as the last paragraph is read aloud, or read it aloud together. How do you personally respond to the merciful judgment of God, who says "Your punishment is this: I forgive you"?

10

Back to the Real World
Revelation 22:6-21

The book closes with an open-ended plea: "Come, Lord Jesus!" We are invited to carry that testimony, but we are unworthy, impure in our actions, and uncertain about what exactly God calls us to do. Yet, in spite of our impurity and uncertainty, we are called to share the compassionate love of Christ with those who hurt. As we offer that healing power of God to a broken world, we, ourselves, are healed.

Personal Preparation
1. Read the passage aloud. Then go back and reread some of your favorite sections of this book.
2. Review the previous nine lessons and list some of the themes that have been especially meaningful to you.
3. How have you been healed by offering God's healing power to others?

Understanding
As we come to the close of Revelation, we see once again a series of tensions that the vision holds together. There is the tension between exclusion and inclusion, heaven and earth, perfection and imperfection, judgment and grace.

In keeping, these closing verses seem both to exclude and to embrace at the same time. The lines between pure and impure are

clearly drawn so we know who's in and who's out. Saint and sinner, evil and righteous, filthy and holy are unmistakably distinguished (22:11, 14-15). Inside the holy city are those whose robes are washed clean (22:14; cf. 3:4-5), and "outside are the dogs and sorcerers and fornicators and murderers and idolaters and everyone who loves and practices falsehood" (22:15). This is a catalogue of those within and outside the church who encourage Christians to engage in idolatrous emperor worship. They are unambiguously wrong, and those who resist them are pure. But in the midst of all this black and white, either/or, us and them language comes the surprisingly universal invitation: "Let everyone who is thirsty come. Let anyone who wishes take the water of life as a gift" (22:17).

This invitation has a double meaning. It is both our invitation to Jesus to be with us and Jesus' invitation to us to come to him. Verse 17 begins as our invitation to Jesus: "The Spirit and the bride say, 'Come.' And let everyone who hears say, 'Come.'" In Greek, the imperative verb *come* is singular. A single person is to be summoned. The Spirit and the bride are to urge Jesus to come (cf. 22:20).

Earlier in Revelation, we saw the "Spirit" as the one who communicates the vision of heaven, who reveals the word of God to the churches. The "bride" elsewhere describes the pure "saints" (19:7-8), the New Jerusalem (21:2), those people who are now ready to join the Lamb and God in unprecedented intimacy (21:2-3). Notice that the "bride" is not simply the church in the here and now. It is rather the redeemed peoples with whom God dwells in the new heaven and new earth (21:3). The "bride" represents the peoples' future, where all things are made new (21:5). The Spirit joins with "the bride" to urge Jesus to come.

The "Spirit" (the churches' power of vision) and the "bride" (the churches' destiny) invite Jesus to the marriage tent for the consummation of their mutual love. Yet even as the Spirit and the bride say "Come," the voice of Jesus is inviting all who are thirsty to come. Anyone who wishes may take the water of life as a free gift. This is Jesus' invitation to us. The call thus issues from earth to heaven and, at the same time, from heaven to earth. The church invites Jesus to come, and Jesus invites anyone who wants to to come. Heaven and earth move toward each other. Our longing for Jesus and Jesus' longing for the world meet in a holy embrace.

But we have to remember that John pictures the reconciliation of heaven and earth in a crystal clear vision that is, as yet, unfulfilled. Here and now, we live in shadowy grays. It is not at all clear when we in the modern world are worshiping idols and rejecting Jesus' invitation. Idols today are not clearly marked. They don't sit in buildings with signs that say Caesar or Roma. We may find ourselves worshiping idols without even knowing it. Instead of wood and stone and candles and incense, idols may be unhealthy relationships, obsessive work, a church building, consumer goods, prestige among peers, or nationalism. The problem is that we cannot avoid these things. We all need relationships, work, meeting places, possessions, a sense of acceptance, a commitment to the larger social good. These are good things and not inherently idolatrous. But in these shadowy grays of history's dusk, it is sometimes hard to make out the lines between what's good about culture and what is idolatrous. It is difficult to know when we have crossed the line and turned the necessary things of life into gods to be worshiped. The dim contours of life in the here and now cannot compare with the brilliant clarity of the New Jerusalem.

If we are honest, then, we would acknowledge that our invitation to Jesus is somewhat ambivalent. By the light of the ever present Lamb, much of our life may be shown to lie outside the walls of New Jerusalem. Our works are not completely pure. As long as we live and participate in systems that are partly good and partly evil, the church stands guilty, tainted, stained, condemned by its own works. Try as we might, we cannot be completely pure in this life. Whether we like it or not, at some level we all drink the wine of "fornication" with "Babylon" (18:3). By our own works, we are judged unprepared for the marriage feast of the Lamb. Our robe is stained.

Our attempts to be faithful are further complicated by our inability even to understand what God asks of us through strange books like Revelation. Throughout history, Christians have interpreted its message in widely varying ways. It has always been highly controversial. How can we, living in the shadowy grays of the here and now, judge its right interpretation?

The second-century "heretic" Montanus thought he had the answer. He was one of the first in a long line of Christian interpreters who have seen in the pages of Revelation a precise prediction of historical events, a cosmic timetable whose conclusion would come in the very near future. Social historians have also noted a pattern of increased apocalyptic expectation at the turn of centuries. And just prior to the turn of the first millennium, apocalyptic movements sprang up all over Christian Europe, comparing the symbolic narrative of Revelation with events in their own day. In times of social and political upheaval, when tried and true beliefs and practices have been thrown into question by rapid and substantial change, when people are uncertain and anxious about the way things are going, Revelation enjoys renewed interest.

In our own era we saw dramatic political change as the Cold War heated up and then collapsed in on itself. With it came a typical rise in apocalyptic thinking. A number of apocalyptic books and movies started to appear in the 1970s, just as detente and warmer relations between the superpowers threatened to unsettle the delicate "peace" of the Cold War. By far, the most popular was Hal Lindsey's book (later made into a movie), *The Late, Great Planet Earth*. This bestseller compared the apocalyptic symbols of Daniel, Ezekiel, Revelation, and other biblical books with cold war political alliances and recent events. Based on his study of this apocalyptic literature, Lindsey predicted a thermonuclear confrontation between the U.S.-led NATO alliance (the forces of God) and the Soviet-led Warsaw Pact (the forces of the antichrist). Israel would be the flashpoint for this final battle of Armageddon.

Ultimately, the international order upon which he based the final battle of good and evil fell apart. The collapse of Eastern bloc communism, the destruction of the Berlin Wall, and dissolution of the Soviet Union into independent, free-market states threw a king-sized monkey wrench into Lindsey's apocalyptic scenario. But the apparent failure of his prediction will do nothing to end such apocalyptic speculation.

We are all shocked by the apocalyptic paranoia of David Koresh, who thought himself to be the God-chosen interpreter of heaven's "seventh seal," a role Revelation reserves for the resurrected Jesus. We were stunned by the murderous apocalypticism of Jim Jones. But these tragedies do not seem to deter people from spinning out end-of-the-world scenarios, especially in periods of rapid and cataclysmic change. Apocalyptic movements are astonishingly persistent in the face of failed predictions, as the histories of the British Watchtower Society (Jehovah's Witnesses) and the Jamaican Rastafarian movement have shown.

Lindsey's mistaken predictions and Koresh's tragic paranoia notwithstanding, we can expect a rise in Revelation-based apocalyptic movements as we enter the year 2000, a new millennium. This turning of the calendar coincides with an uncertain international order, environmental crises, and rapidly evolving information technologies. All these things carry with them dramatic social, economic, and political consequences—rapid and sometimes breathtaking change. The next several years will be intensely uncertain, exciting, challenging, and frightening: fertile ground for apocalyptic speculation.

So what must the church do with Revelation? Should we heed the advice of Eusebius, Cyril of Jerusalem, Martin Luther, Ulrich Zwingli, and others and put Revelation in a dark corner in the closet? Is it too dangerous to be of use for Christian thought and action? Even if we can overcome Revelation's tragic misuse over the centuries and discover its word for us today, can the church possibly bear up under the weight of its uncompromising call? What is the impure, uncertain church to do? How may an unholy church, such as we are, bear the holy testimony of God?

In his book *When Bad Things Happen to Good People*, Rabbi Harold Kushner tells an ancient Chinese story about a woman whose only son died. She went to a holy man for magic to bring her son back to life. The holy man said that he could not restore her son, but he could help her with the pain of her grief. He sent her to find a mustard seed from a home which had never known sorrow. The seed would be the chief ingredient in a potion to relieve her grief. Quickly, she began her quest. From the most splendid mansion to the poorest hovel, she searched for the seed, but everywhere she found stories of deep pain and sorrow. At each home, she stayed for a while to comfort the people there. In the end, the woman became so involved in caring for the grief stricken that she forgot all about her quest for the mustard seed, never realizing that the quest itself had driven away her own sorrow.

The church is an impure vessel, uncertain and unworthy to carry the pure testimony it has been given. Perhaps it is only as we bear the testimony of Jesus to a broken, impure, unwhole world that we come to experience our own healing. At the end of Daniel's apocalyptic vision, the angelic messenger told Daniel to "keep the words secret and the book sealed until the time of the end" (Dan. 12:4). John is told the opposite: "Do not seal up the words of the prophecy of this book, for the time is near" (22:10). The message is open to all. The invitation is universal. And the witness of the church is the way the call of Jesus is issued: "Let everyone who is thirsty come. Let anyone who wishes take the water of life as a gift" (22:17).

As we offer the healing water of God to a hurting world, we ourselves are healed. As we bring the thirsty a drink of God's pure water, we ourselves are purified. And, though still imperfect, uncertain, and unwhole, we can greet with celebration the assurance of the one who calls us: "Surely I am coming soon." Amen! Come, Lord Jesus!

Discussion and Action

1. Read aloud Revelation 22:6-21. Listen as three or four people read these verses from the same translation. Or share Bibles so all can read aloud together.
2. Talk about what it means when we say "Come, Lord Jesus." What does it mean for you personally? What does it mean for the church? What does it mean for the world?
3. Think of times or places where we foul things up even though we have the best intentions. But often those foul-ups somehow work out in the end. Share a few such instances. What made things go wrong? What made them go right?
4. When have you found yourself healed as you were offering help to someone else?
5. Name situations in your own life, the church, and the larger society that especially need the healing presence of Christ. What can you do as a group or as individuals to invite Jesus to be present?
6. Pray as a group for the continued presence and healing power of Jesus among you as you bring this study to a close.

Suggestions for Sharing and Prayer

This material is designed for covenant groups that spend an hour in sharing and praying together, in addition to the hour of Bible study. These suggestions will help to relate the group's sharing to their study of *Revelation: Hope for the World in Troubled Times*. Session-by-session ideas are given, followed by general resources. This guide was compiled by June Adams Gibble, of Elgin, Illinois, and Suzanne DeMoss Martin, of Indianapolis, Indiana.

1. Let Those Who Have Ears Hear

❏ Talk about something from childhood that once seemed very mysterious to you (where the meaning was almost hidden), but later became clear. Enjoy listening to each other's stories.

❏ Share with the group some of the events in your life that you recalled during personal preparation, events that came to have a greater significance than you knew at the time.

❏ Recall some of your earliest memories of what Revelation was about; share these around the group. Then, as a group, make a list of the stories, the images, the characters, and the songs that you know are found in the book of Revelation. Add to this list throughout your study.

❏ What are your hopes, what do you anticipate, as you begin this study of Revelation? What are your anxieties about this study? Have one person jot these down as they are named.

❏ Bring to God in prayer all of these hopes, anticipations, anxieties. Have one person offer the prayer on behalf of all; or individuals may offer sentence prayers.

❏ Consider choosing prayer partners. Covenant with each other to pray together for understanding throughout your study of Revelation; pray that you and your group will be open to God's word for you today.

2. A Vision of Christ in the Church's Night

❏ Invite people to recall an early childhood dream:
Who was in your dream?
What were they wearing?
Where did it take place?
What sounds and feelings did you experience?
What happened, what was the outcome?
Take time to remember and then ask people to share their dreams.

❏ Recall times you sang the song "Jacob's Ladder" (in summer camps, Sunday school, youth groups, at vespers). Recognize that this song is based on a biblical dream, when God was present with Jacob.

❏ Share times when you've experienced the presence of God in a particularly strong way, in a dream, a vision, at worship, or in some other way.

❏ Invite people to silently think of times when they have felt the Spirit of God "fall upon" them or the congregation during a service of worship. Share with the group as people choose.

❏ Sing as a closing prayer "Spirit of the Living God." Sing it a second time using the word *us* in place of *me*.

3. Rendering to Caesar

❏ Tell about the symbol you chose in your personal preparation to describe your church and why that symbol seems appropriate to you.

❏ Mark on a map the locations of the seven churches named in Revelation 2—3. Keep this image before you as you discuss the messages to these churches.

❏ Assign one of these churches to each person. In reading about each church in Revelation 2—3, look for the diagnosis (what's wrong), the treatment (what to do), and the prognosis (what God promises, what can/will happen).

For example, consider the church at Sardis:
The diagnosis: The church is dead, or at least on its deathbed.
The treatment: Remember what you have heard. Wake up!
The prognosis: There is still time for those who repent.

❏ Talk about the problems of the seven churches and any of these problems present in your own congregation. What is the promise, the word of hope, you need to hear?

❏ Pray with your prayer partner for your congregation, your denomination, and all of God's church around the world; pray for specific people and situations where you know there is a need.

❏ Close by singing a hymn for the church, such as "I Love Thy Kingdom, Lord" or "The Church's One Foundation."

4. Being There

❏ Sing "I Know Not Why God's Wondrous Grace" (p. 75), "He's Got the Whole World In His Hands," "O God, Our Help in Ages Past," or hymns that celebrate God's presence in the midst of an uncertain future.

❏ Talk about some of the uncertainties in your life right now. How is God a part of them? Where do you find hope?

❏ As a group, chant together verses 4:8b, 11; 5:9-10, 12, 13b. Or try chanting these verses responsively, with two groups responding to each other. Bring in rhythm instruments to use with your chanting and singing of Revelation's songs and hymns; you could use tambourines, drums, castanets, maracas, among others.

❏ Listen to selections from Handel's *Messiah*, especially "The Hallelujah Chorus," and try singing along with the music.

❑ Sing the doxology. Learn it in a new form, "Praise God from Whom All Blessings Flow" (p. 77). Encourage your congregation or choir to sing this in worship.

❑ Pray together as you sing favorite hymns of adoration and praise. Close your prayer time by singing a threefold or fivefold "Amen."

5. How Long, O Lord?

❑ Read together, chant together, or read responsively Revelation 7:5-8, 10, 12, 15-17. Do this at least two or three times. What do you think these words and phrases meant to a young and persecuted church?

❑ Share the many places where you have seen evidence of evil, persecution, or injustice this week (on television, in newspapers or magazines, in people's actions). In such a world as this, where is the hope?

❑ Pray the lament psalm, Psalm 13. First, have people read it silently, prayerfully. Next, read it aloud in unison as your prayer. Finally, pray it together, changing the words *me/my/I* to *us/our/we*.

6. Bittersweet Words

❑ Name some common (and perhaps fun) things in life that are bittersweet (such as bitter cough medicine that does stop the coughing).

❑ Talk about where you have found hope in the midst of "bittersweet struggles."

❑ Read together or chant Revelation 11:15b, recognizing that these words are part of Handel's *Messiah*. Listen to a recording of this music and sing along with it.

❑ Look for praise hymns in your hymnal. Find the images and phrases that come directly from the words of praise in

Revelation. Keep a list of these hymns throughout your
study of Revelation.

❑ Focus your prayer time around the words of the hymn "Here
I Am, Lord" (p. 81). Practice singing the refrain together.
Listen then as one person reads the words or sings the first
stanza, then respond with the refrain; continue through
the hymn.

❑ With your prayer partner, talk about the bittersweet
situations depicted in this hymn; then pray for each other.
Close with the whole group singing the words of the refrain
of "Here I Am, Lord," adding "Amen."

7. In the Clutches of the Beast

❑ Tell about your experiences with fasting during the week.

❑ Talk about other kinds of fasting (from radio or television,
from telephones, from specific foods such as chocolate).
Covenant with prayer partners to fast in some special way in
the coming week.

❑ Talk about some of the beasts in old fairy tales, children's
stories, and movies, including both the "good beasts" and the
"bad beasts." What are some of the "beasts" that plague your
life today?

❑ Let Martin Luther's hymn "A Mighty Fortress Is Our God"
speak to you. Read the words together, listen while one
person reads each stanza, or listen while one or several
people sing the hymn.

❑ In a prayer circle, pray for people and situations around the
world. Invite the participants to name their concerns, with
the group responding after each intercession with the words
"Hear our prayer, O God" or "Be with your people, O God."

❑ Close by singing the majestic hymn "A Mighty Fortress Is
Our God."

8. God Is Victorious

❑ Choose from the following scriptures to read or chant together: Revelation 18:10b, 14, 16-17, 19b-20, 21b-24; 19:1b-3, 5b, 6b-8. Again, consider accompanying your chanting with rhythm instruments or by clapping your hands.

❑ What can you as members of a covenant group do to begin living out of a different vision? Name some specific things; then covenant with each other to do at least one of them.

❑ Pray Psalm 51:1-4, 10-12 with prayer partners:

   a. Each person read the first four verses silently, prayerfully, and reflect on the words.

   b. Then read verses 10-12 silently, and reflect on them.

   c. As prayer partners, pray these words together quietly.

   d. Pray the psalm together again, this time using the words *us/our/we* instead of *me/my/I*.

❑ Sing your closing prayer together as a covenant group: "Into my heart, into my heart, come into my heart, Lord Jesus. Come in today. Come in to stay. Come into my heart, Lord Jesus."

9. Judgment at the Mercy Seat

❑ Share some of the times you expected to be punished and instead were surprised by mercy. Come together in prayer as you sing "Amazing Grace," recognizing and accepting God's mercy.

❑ Close your eyes and listen as one member of the group reads Revelation 21:1-4. Visualize what this new world, the "new heaven and new earth," will look like. As this becomes clear to you, use crayons or paint or clay to create an image of your vision.

❑ Share both visions and creations with your prayer partner; then, as you choose, share these with the whole group.

❑ Read the words of the hymn "Beyond a Dying Sun" (p. 83). Learn this hymn by "lining" it: one person sings phrases one and two, and the group repeats them; then one person sings phrases three and four, with the group responding; then all sing the refrain. Learn all the stanzas in this way.

❑ Plan to teach this hymn to the congregation, using the method of "lining" the hymn.

10. Back to the Real World

❑ What are your favorite parts of Revelation? Read them aloud to each other.

❑ Share some times in your life when these words from Revelation have spoken to you in an important way.

❑ Recall some of your anxieties and fears as you began this study of Revelation. Is anything different now? What have been your new learnings from the study?

❑ In this last sharing time, you may want to sing again some of the hymns that you have enjoyed throughout your study.

❑ Read together as a group the last paragraph of the Understanding section. Close by praying for each member of your group by name; or have a simple anointing service (see p. 74).

General Sharing and Prayer Resources

A Gathering Prayer

Gather us, God, to be with you as you are with us.
As our Nigerian brothers and sisters say,
it is *abin mamaki* [ah BIN ma MAK ee—a thing of wonder]
to journey to this moment, to stand in this place before you:
Creator, Sustainer, Redeemer.

Help us to hear your promise and know its truth:
"Here and now I will do a new thing;
this moment it will break from the bud."

Gather us, God, to be with each other as you are with each of us.
It is *abin mamaki* to enter into treasured ritual, into prayer,
with sisters and brothers.

Gather us, God. Amen.

By Judith G. Kipp. Used by permission.

A Call to Worship

This is a time of worship,
    a time for knowing that there is a Power beyond our own,
    that it is God who has made us and not we ourselves.
This is a time of prayer,
    a time for bringing ourselves, just as we are,
    into the presence of the Holy One.
This is a time of praise,
    a time for lifting our hearts and voices
    in grateful thanksgiving to our Maker.

By Kenneth L. Gibble. Used by permission.

An Affirmation of Faith

Let us say what we believe.
We believe in God, the Holy One who created all things.
We believe that God was in Jesus Christ,
    drawing the world back to God.
We believe that God is still creating,
    judging, and saving the world God loves.
We believe that the living Christ is present among us,
    giving us hope, courage, and peace.
With God's help, we will live out our beliefs
    with courage and compassion.

By Kenneth L. Gibble. Used by permission.

An Affirmation for Ending Worship

One: We live in God's present kingdom,
    and we look forward to that kingdom's coming
        in its fullness.

All: Life in the kingdom is not solitary life;
    we walk hand in hand with our brothers and sisters.

One: Christ is our guide on the journey.
    He is our example; his living presence goes with us.

All: With Christ and in the glad company of the kingdom folk,
    we walk with courage and hope. May God be praised!

By Kenneth L. Gibble. Used by permission.

A Prayer for Light in Darkness

Luminous God,
    the truth of our lives
    is that there is much to frighten us:
        fears of illness, debilitating health
        nightmares of disaster, warring madness
        bleak hopelessness, consuming hurts.

Awaken us, O Christ,
    and turn our truth to
        daring the hard work of love
        shedding the light of commitment and joy
        following the Prince of Peace.

Luminous God,
    Awaken us out of our sleep.
    Raise us up
        sparkling
        glimmering
        shining
        and radiant.
            Amen.

By Judith G. Kipp. Used by permission.

A Prayer

O God, you rule the world from end to end
    and for all time.
You alone are God. In you alone we hope.

Forgive our sins.
Heal our diseases.
Save our lives from destruction.

We repent of our stubbornness and pride.
We desire to yield ourselves more fully to your will.

Keep us in your presence
    that we might serve and witness in the world,
    through Jesus Christ, our Lord. Amen.

Source unknown.

A Prayer Resource

Encourage members of the covenant group to use *A World at Prayer: The New Ecumenical Prayer Cycle*, published by Twenty-Third Publications, Mystic, Connecticut, 1990 (800 321-0411). This book contains prayers, hymns, litanies, and reflections from people in many countries around the world, with resources from a group of countries for each of 52 weeks. Group members may use these materials for praying at home; and the covenant group will find this book a rich resource for their prayer life together.

Anoint Us, O God

Within us is a yearning
   for healing, wholeness, blessing,
     and peace.

With You is the turning
   to restoration, wisdom, strengthening,
     and grace.

We gather now the ordinary things:
   oil, people, words,
     and time.

Make possible the impossible!

Lead us out of our sin
   pain, grief
     and weariness.

Anoint us now, O God.

By Judith G. Kipp. Used by permission.

An Anointing Service

The service of anointing, as practiced by the Church of the Brethren, is based on the biblical practice of anointing for healing; James 5:13-16 is a basic text. More information is available in an anointing packet available from Brethren Press, 800 441-3712.

A simple anointing service includes:
Personal indication of need and request for anointing;
James 5:13-16 text;
Brief words about God's will for wholeness of body, mind, spirit;
An opportunity for confession, for seeking peace with God;
An assurance of pardon;
The anointing with oil.

> Brief words are spoken during the anointing, such as:
> Upon your confession of faith and your
> willingness to commit your life to God,
> you are anointed with oil for the forgive-
> ness of sin, for the strengthening of faith,
> and for healing and wholeness according
> to God's grace and wisdom.

> The pastor or leader puts a few drops of oil on his or her own finger(s) and touches the afflicted person's forehead three times, once as each purpose is stated. Then the pastor or leader places hands lightly on the anointed person's head and offers prayers.

I know not why God's wondrous

I know not why God's won - drous grace to me he
I know not how this sav - ing faith to me he
I know not how the Spir - it moves, con - vinc - ing
I know not when my Lord may come, at night or

hath made known, nor why, with mer - cy, Christ in love re -
did im - part, nor how be - liev - ing in his word wrought
us of sin, re - veal - ing Je - sus through the word, cre -
noon - day fair, nor if I'll walk the vale with him, or

Refrain

deemed me for his own.
peace with - in my heart. But I know whom I have be -
at - ing faith in him.
meet him in the air.

liev - ed, and am per - suad - ed that he is a - ble to

Text: Daniel W. Whittle, *Gospel Hymns, No. 4*, 1883, alt.
Music: James McGranahan, *Gospel Hymns, No. 4*, 1883

keep that which I've com - mit - ted un - to him a - gainst that day.

Praise God from whom

*Alternate phrases: Praise God from whom all blessings flow, praise God all creatures here below, praise God above, ye heav'nly host

Text: Thomas Ken, *Manual of Prayers for the Use of Scholars of Winchester College*, 1695, altered 1709
Music: Boston Handel and Haydn Society Collection ..., 1830

*Alternate phrase: O praise our God, bless'd Three-in-One

Here I am, Lord

1. I, the Lord of sea and sky,
   I have heard my people cry.
   All who dwell in dark and sin
   my hand will save.
   I who made the stars of night,
   I will make their darkness bright.
   Who will bear my light to them?
   Whom shall I send?
   (Refrain)

2. I, the Lord of snow and rain,
   I have borne my people's pain.
   I have wept for love of them.
   They turn away.
   I will break their hearts of stone,
   give them hearts for love alone.
   I will speak my word to them.
   Whom shall I send?
   (Refrain)

3. I, the Lord of wind and flame,
   I will tend the poor and lame.
   I will set a feast for them.
   My hand will save.
   Finest bread I will provide,
   till their hearts be satisfied.
   I will give my life to them.
   Whom shall I send?
   (Refrain)

Text: based on Isaiah 6, Daniel Schutte, 1980, *Lord of Light*, 1981
Music: Daniel Schutte; arranged by Michael Pope, SJ, and John Weissrock

Here I am, Lord

1 I, the Lord of sea and sky,
I have heard my people cry.
All who dwell in dark and
my hand will save.
I who made the stars of
I will make their darkness
Who will bear my light to
Whom shall I send?
(Refrain)

2 I, the Lord of snow and rain,
I have borne my people's
I have wept for love of them.
They turn away.
I will brake their hearts of
give them hearts for love
I will speak my word to
Whom shall I send?
(Refrain)

3 I, the Lord of wind and
I will tend the poor and
I will set a feast for them.
My hand will save.
Finest bread I will provide,
till their hearts be satisfied.
I will give my life to them.
Whom shall I send?
(Refrain)

Text: based on Isaiah 6, Daniel Schutte, 1980, *Lord of Light*, 1981
Music: Daniel Schutte; arranged by Michael Pope, SJ, and John Weissrock

Beyond a dying sun

Text: Steve Engle, 1970; revised 1984
Music: Steve Engle, 1970; harmonized by Don Frederick and Steve Engle
Text and Music copyright © 1970 Steve Engle and the Church of the Brethren, LaVerne, CA

Refrain

I see a new world com - ing when ev - 'ry-one is free! And

all shall be God's peo - ple in jus - tice, love and peace.

Other Covenant Bible Studies available from *faithQuest:*